JAMES COOK

The Voyages

JAMES COOK

The Voyages

William Frame with Laura Walker

McGill-Queen's University Press
Montreal & Kingston / Chicago

ISBN 978-0-7735-5286-9 (cloth)
ISBN 978-0-7735-5404-7 (ePDF)

Legal deposit second quarter 2018
Bibliothèque nationale du Québec

Published simultaneously outside North America by the British Library

Printed in China

Funded by the Government of Canada | Financé par le gouvernement du Canada | Canada

Canada Council for the Arts | Conseil des arts du Canada

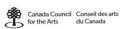

We acknowledge the support of the Canada Council for the Arts, which last year invested $153 million to bring the arts to Canadians throughout the country. Nous remercions le Conseil des arts du Canada de son soutien. L'an dernier, le Conseil a investi 153 millions de dollars pour mettre de l'art dans la vie des Canadiennes et des Canadiens de tout le pays.

Library and Archives Canada Cataloguing in Publication

Frame, William, 1972–, author
James Cook : the voyages / William Frame with Laura Walker.

Includes bibliographical references and index.
Issued in print and electronic formats.
ISBN 978-0-7735-5286-9 (cloth).–ISBN 978-0-7735-5404-7 (ePDF)

1. Cook, James, 1728–1779 – Travel – Pacific Area. 2. Explorers – Great Britain – Biography. 3. Voyages around the world – History – 18th century. 4. Natural history – History – 18th century. 5. Travel in art. 6. Pacific Area – Discovery and exploration – British. 7. Oceania – Discovery and exploration – British. I. Walker, Laura, 1986–, author II. Title.

G420.C65F73 2018 910.9182'3 C2017-907539-X
C2017-907540-3

Designed by Will Webb

CONTENTS

A Note on the Text

This book uses primary sources, including journals, artworks and maps, to tell the story of James Cook's three voyages of exploration. The approach is broadly chronological, but we have used individual documents and images to explore particular episodes or themes in more detail. The nature of the sources means that in most cases the bulk of the evidence is presented from a British perspective. In the text, we have tried to indicate some of the problems of interpretation this brings.

The modern English forms of personal and place names are used, except in quotations, where the original spelling is followed. Where there is no agreed modern form, we have tried to use the most commonly accepted spelling. The spelling in original quotations has been retained, including both the many eighteenth-century variations in style and the equally common spelling and grammatical errors. By making extensive use of the words of contemporaries, the book aims to show how eight-eenth-century European ideas about non-European cultures shaped the story of the voyages. Needless to say, our purpose is to document these views, not to endorse them.

British naval tradition defined each day as running from midday to midday, so that journal entries for a particular date often relate to the afternoon of one day and the morning of the next. On the other hand, some of the civilians on board ship continued to use standard dating during the voyage. We have used the date given in the individual journal in each case. We have not included references for journal quotations but have provided the dates of entries in the text, to make it easier for readers who may wish to follow them up. The more readily available printed and online editions of journals are listed in the bibliography.

The captions for images include references to the original sources. Where titles of artworks and maps are given in quotation marks this indicates a commonly used title. Where titles are given in square brackets this indicates a title based on a description of the work.

John Webber,
'A Young Woman of Otaheite,
bringing a Present', 1777
British Library, Add MS 15513, f. 17

Acknowledgements

The wide-ranging nature of this book and the complexity surrounding much of the storyline means that we have drawn on the work of many previous writers and researchers. We have listed the works we found most helpful in the further reading section at the end of the book.

Many people have provided help, advice and encouragement during the course of writing this book and preparing the accompanying exhibition. In particular, we would like to thank: Robyn Allardice-Bourne, Louise Anemaat, Ben Appleton, Sir David Attenborough, Alexandra Ault, Marie-Louise Ayres, Howard Batho, Michael Budden, Andrea Clarke, Rob Davies, Silvia Dobrovich, Tabitha Driver, Nick Dykes, Susan Dymond, Lars Eckstein, Layla Fedyk, Robin Frame, Alex Hailey, Tom Harper, Andrea Hart, Susannah Helman, Peter Hooker, Marcie Hopkins, Carolyn Jones, Alex Lock, John McAleer, Scot McKendrick, Mary McMahon, Margaret Makepeace, Kate Marshall, Elizabeth Martindale, Sir Jerry Mateparae, Alex Michaels, Fraser Muggeridge, the members of Ngāti Rānana London Māori Club, Camilla Nichol, Stephen Noble, Maria Nugent, Andra Patterson, Maggie Patton, Helen Peden, Magdalena Peszko, Ben Pollitt, Martha Rawlinson, Nigel Rigby, Huw Rowlands, Emma Scanlan, Anja Schwarz, Gaye Sculthorpe, Matthew Shaw, Geoff Shearcroft, Nicholas Thomas, Cliff Thornton, Sandra Tuppen, Michael Turner, Jo Walsh, Martin Woods, Janet Zmroczek. Any remaining errors of fact or interpretation are the responsibility of the authors.

Many institutions have provided help, either through lending original collection items to the exhibition or through the provision of advice and support. We would like to thank: the Museum of Archaeology and Anthropology, Cambridge; the National Library of Australia, Canberra; the National Archives, Kew; the National Portrait Gallery, London; the Natural History Museum, London; the Captain Cook Memorial Museum, Whitby; the Royal College of Surgeons, London; the Royal Armouries, Leeds; the Royal Collection, Windsor; the Royal Society, London; the State Library of New South Wales, Sydney; the UK Antarctic Heritage Trust, Cambridge; the University Museum of Zoology, Cambridge; the Whipple Museum of the History of Science, Cambridge.

MAPS

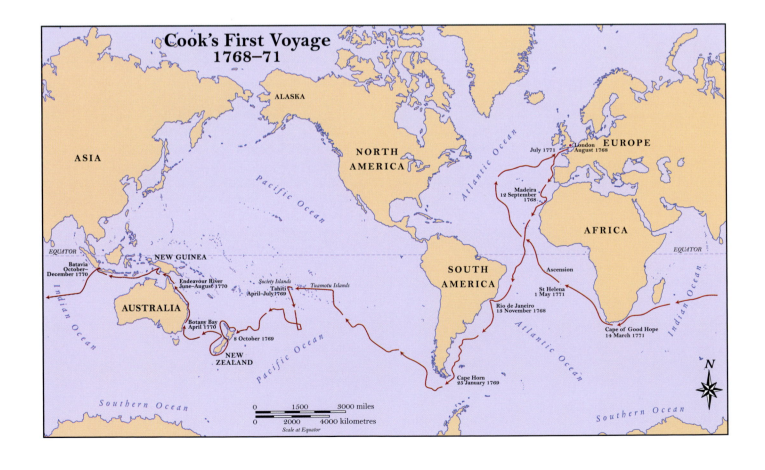

Cook's First Voyage 1768–71

ALASKA

ASIA

NORTH AMERICA

Pacific Ocean

Atlantic Ocean

July 1771 • London August 1768 EUROPE

Madeira 12 September 1768

AFRICA

EQUATOR

EQUATOR

NEW GUINEA

Batavia October–December 1770

Endeavour River June–August 1770

Society Islands Tahiti April–July 1769 *Tuamotu Islands*

Ascension

SOUTH AMERICA

St Helena 1 May 1771

AUSTRALIA

Botany Bay April 1770

8 October 1769

NEW ZEALAND

Rio de Janeiro 13 November 1768

Cape of Good Hope 14 March 1771

Indian Ocean

Indian Ocean

Pacific Ocean

Atlantic Ocean

Cape Horn 25 January 1769

N

Southern Ocean

Southern Ocean

0   1500   3000 miles
0   2000   4000 kilometres
Scale at Equator

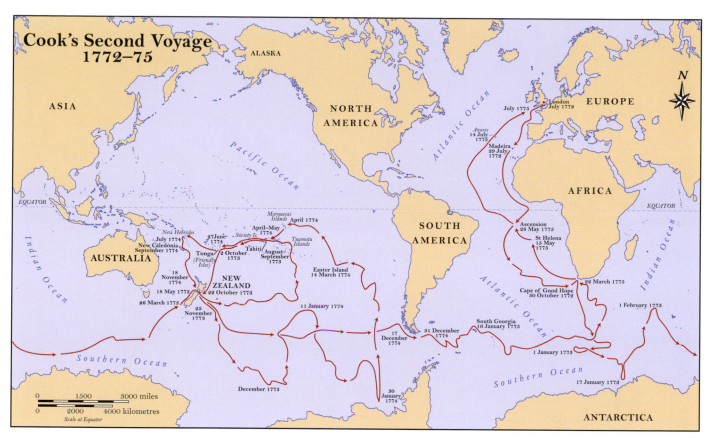

Cook's Second Voyage
1772–75

ALASKA

ASIA

NORTH
AMERICA

EUROPE

Atlantic Ocean

London
July 1772

July 1775

Azores
14 July
1775

Madeira
29 July
1772

AFRICA

EQUATOR

Pacific Ocean

EQUATOR

SOUTH
AMERICA

Ascension
28 May 1775

St Helena
15 May
1775

Indian Ocean

*Marquesas
Islands* April 1774

April–May
1774

Society Is.

New Hebrides
July 1774

27 June
1774

New Caledonia
September 1774

*Tuamotu
Islands*

Tahiti
August–
September
1773

AUSTRALIA

Tonga
(*Friendly
Isles*)

2 October
1773

Easter Island
14 March 1774

22 March 1775

Cape of Good Hope
30 October 1772

1 February 1775

18
November
1774

NEW
ZEALAND

22 October 1773

Atlantic Ocean

18 May 1773

26 March 1773

25
November
1773

11 January 1774

17
December
1774

31 December
1774

South Georgia
16 January 1775

1 January 1775

December 1773

30
January
1774

Southern Ocean

Southern Ocean

17 January 1775

	1500		3000 miles
0			
	2000		4000 kilometres
0			
Scale at Equator

ANTARCTICA

N

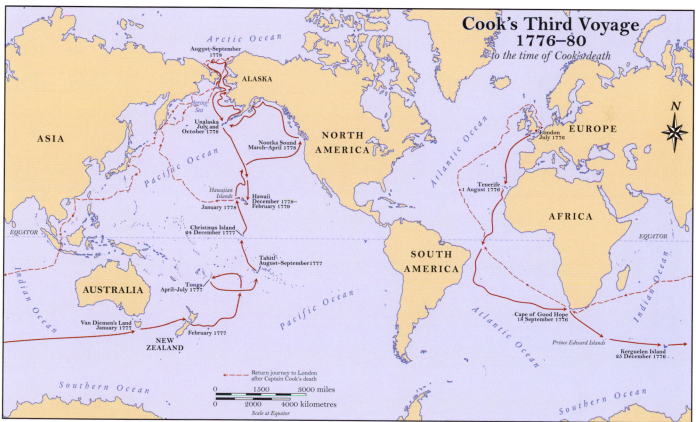

Cook's Third Voyage
1776–80
to the time of Cook's death

Arctic Ocean

August–September
1778

ALASKA

*Bering
Sea*

ASIA

Unalaska
July and
October 1778

Nootka Sound
March–April 1778

NORTH
AMERICA

Pacific Ocean

EUROPE

London
July 1776

Atlantic Ocean

Tenerife
1 August 1776

*Hawaiian
Islands*

January 1778

Hawaii
December 1778–
February 1779

AFRICA

Christmas Island
24 December 1777

EQUATOR

EQUATOR

Tahiti
August–September 1777

SOUTH
AMERICA

Tonga
April–July 1777

AUSTRALIA

Pacific Ocean

Indian Ocean

Cape of Good Hope
18 September 1776

Van Diemen's Land
January 1777

February 1777

NEW
ZEALAND

Prince Edward Islands

Kerguelen Island
25 December 1776

Atlantic Ocean

Southern Ocean

- - - Return journey to London
after Captain Cook's death

	1500		3000 miles
0			
	2000		4000 kilometres
0			
Scale at Equator

Southern Ocean

N

E. Phillips Fox,
*Landing of Captain Cook
at Botany Bay, 1770*, 1902,
oil on canvas
National Gallery of Victoria,
Melbourne

INTRODUCTION

The three voyages of James Cook spanned more than a decade, from 1768, when the *Endeavour* sailed from Plymouth, to 1780, when the *Resolution* and *Discovery* returned to Britain after Cook's death in Hawai'i. The initial aim of the *Endeavour* voyage was to record the transit of Venus at Tahiti, in order to calculate the distance from the Earth to the Sun, and all three voyages included scientific goals in their planning. However, the main motivation behind the Admiralty's support for the voyages was the search for land, notably the Great Southern Continent believed to lie somewhere in the southern oceans, and for new commercial and trading opportunities. Cook's ships visited many places that were new or unfamiliar to Europeans, including Tahiti, New Zealand, the east coast of Australia, the Antarctic, Easter Island, Tonga, Vanuatu (the New Hebrides), South Georgia, Hawai'i, the Pacific Northwest, Alaska and the Bering Sea.

The voyages followed almost 250 years of European exploration of the Pacific. In 1520 the Portuguese navigator Ferdinand Magellan, exploring on behalf of the Spanish Crown, had led the first European expedition to cross the Pacific. The English, in the form of privateers such as Sir Francis Drake and William Dampier, had made sporadic forays into the Pacific in the sixteenth and seventeenth centuries. The Portuguese, approaching from their territories in the Indian Ocean, had also begun to enter the Pacific during this period. Dutch navigators, including Abel Tasman, began to explore there after the establishment of colonies by the Dutch East India Company in present-day Indonesia in the early seventeenth century. European exploration was accompanied by the claiming of lands, which were often named for the home country. Thus Drake claimed the west coast of North America, calling it New Albion, while on Dutch maps the gradually emerging outline of Australia was called New Holland.

Despite these earlier voyages, when the *Endeavour* set out in 1768 large parts of the Pacific remained unknown in Europe.

Cook was a skilled cartographer and the maps and charts he completed during the voyage were often the first accurate surveys of the coastlines he visited. By the end of the third voyage the map of the world's inhabited coastlines, at least in rough outline, was close to completion. Later the voyages, and Cook himself, became symbolic of much larger changes that took place over the next hundred years. The establishment in 1788 of a penal colony at Sydney Cove was the first step in the British colonisation of Australia. In 1803 a second settlement was established in Van Diemen's Land (Tasmania) and during the nineteenth century colonies were established in other parts of Australia. New Zealand was annexed by the British Crown in 1840. The Commonwealth of Australia was created at Federation in 1901.

In Victorian Britain, Cook was enshrined in the pantheon of inspirational imperial heroes killed in the line of duty. His story became a staple of school assemblies, being told and retold to generations of children until well into the second half of the twentieth century. History textbooks emphasised the role of Cook in establishing the British Empire in the Pacific. In illustrations he was often shown planting the flag at Botany Bay. Alongside figures such as 'Clive of India' and 'Wolfe of Quebec' he became symbolic of the British Empire in a particular area of the world. He was elevated to the role of founding father of Australia and, to a lesser extent, New Zealand, and was celebrated in monuments, statues, street names and postage stamps. The anniversaries of his landings were often commemorated in re-enactments, emphasising the belief that his arrival was the point at which the national story began.

The decades after the Second World War saw a reaction against this version of history. The history of European empires, much of it promulgated by European empire-builders, came under increasingly critical scrutiny during the period of de-colonisation. The story of the English (and later the British)

We Call Them Pirates Out Here

challenge to the over-mighty Catholic powers of Spain, Portugal and France, so much a staple of British education, came to be seen as merely a squabble among thieves over lands belonging to non-European peoples. The idea of the civilising mission of Empire (in Kipling's phrase, the 'white man's burden') came to be seen as a cover for the economic exploitation of subject peoples and lands. Inextricably linked to the history of colonialism was the use of pseudo-scientific racial theories to argue for the superiority of white Europeans over colonised peoples. In Australia, a symbolic moment came in 1970, during the bicentennial celebrations of Cook's arrival at Botany Bay, when

Aboriginal protesters on the opposite shore laid wreaths in the water to commemorate those killed during British colonisation.

As the narrative of European 'discovery' became increasingly challenged, greater interest was taken in the original human settlement of the Pacific. Modern archaeology, allied to sophisticated scientific techniques including carbon dating and DNA analysis, began to uncover the history of human migration, showing how modern humans (*Homo sapiens*) originated in Africa and how around 100,000 years ago they began to migrate from North Africa to the Middle East, from where Asia, Europe and Australasia would be gradually

Daniel Boyd,
We Call Them Pirates
Out Here, 2006, oil on canvas
Museum of Contemporary Art,
Sydney

populated. Although dates remain only estimates, it is believed that *Homo sapiens* reached the Americas around 15,000 years ago, crossing from Asia to Alaska at a time when water levels in the North Pacific were lower than they are now. Exploration and settlement of non-coastal Pacific islands began later, with the remoter islands settled less than 2,000 years ago. New Zealand, far to the south, was the last major landmass to be settled, around 700–800 years ago.

The records of Cook's voyages are now studied as much for the light they shed on societies in the Pacific at the time of early European contact as for the stories they tell of European exploration. Although leading a series of naval expeditions, Cook was accompanied by scientists, including Sir Joseph Banks on the first voyage and Johann Forster on the second voyage. The role of Banks in recruiting a party of artists and scientists to travel to the Pacific established a pattern that would be followed by future expeditions. Many of the officers and scientists on board kept journals, and thousands of pages of manuscript and printed accounts exist describing the voyages. In this way the story of Cook's expeditions fits alongside the stories of figures such as Charles Darwin, whose journey on the *Beagle* was part of a British government surveying expedition that mixed scientific, commercial and imperial goals, or Robert Falcon Scott, another naval officer, whose expeditions combined scientific research with the patriotic attempt to be first to the South Pole.

The British Library holds many of the original maps, artworks and journals from Cook's three voyages. These include Cook's journals for the second and third voyages, many of the maps he created and much of the original artwork by the artists who sailed on the voyages. This book, and the exhibition it accompanies, uses these collections to explore the story of the voyages. In doing so it does not tell a new story or bring to light surprising or previously unknown facts. Rather, by returning to the original sources, it allows many of the protagonists to speak for themselves. The nature of the surviving sources means that these primarily tell the story from the European perspective. Nonetheless, in the thousands of pages of manuscript and printed accounts are buried the voices of many lesser-known participants, both from Europe and from the Pacific. If the original sources contain many gaps and, on occasion, intentional or unintentional distortions, they also allow us to view the voyages as they took place from the perspective of those who were involved.

Cook's voyages still attract both huge interest and fierce controversy. They remain important and relevant to many people. The anniversaries of the voyages, starting in August 2018, 250 years after the *Endeavour* sailed from Plymouth, and extending to autumn 2030, 250 years after the return of the *Resolution* and *Discovery*, offer an extended opportunity to look again at this story. A list of original sources and recent books on the subject is provided at the end of the book, for those who wish to explore the story in more detail. It is hoped that this book and exhibition will help to encourage new research into the stories of the voyages and their significance today. The interconnection between past and present, the way the telling of well-known stories adapts and evolves over time, is a subject that could fill many books. The events of 250 years ago are inextricably linked to what has happened since. While the original sources remain the same, their interpretation continues to evolve.

EIGHTEENTH-CENTURY BRITAIN
The World of James Cook and Joseph Banks

The Kingdom of Great Britain

James Cook's three voyages to the Pacific took place during a period of growing British imperial and economic expansion. The Kingdom of Great Britain had formally come into being in 1707, following the passing of the Acts of Union by the parliament of England and Wales and the parliament of Scotland. The accession of George III in 1760 was a symbolic moment in the development of British national identity. Unlike George I and George II, who were both born in Germany, George III was born in London and spoke English as his first language. In his coronation speech he proclaimed: 'Born and educated in this country, I glory in the name of Britain. The peculiar happiness of my life will ever consist in promoting the welfare of a people whose loyalty and warm affection to me, I consider, as the greatest and most permanent security of my Throne'.

In 1760 Britain was in the middle of its third major war against France since the Act of Union. The Seven Years' War, which broke out in 1756 and lasted until 1763, has been described as the 'first world war'. Campaigns for the control of trade and territories were fought by the British and their allies against the French and their allies in Europe, India and the Americas. Both countries had trading stations on the Indian coast and growing settlements in North America. In India the victories of Robert Clive led to the founding of what became the British Raj. In Canada, where the French had settled along the St Lawrence River, establishing trading posts and the towns of Quebec and Montreal, their defeat led to British hegemony.

In his speech George III described commerce as 'that great source of our Riches'. In eighteenth-century Britain trade was often cited as a central element in national success and, by extension, national identity. The Articles of Union had provided for 'full Freedom and Intercourse of Trade and Navigation, to and from any Port or Place within the said united Kingdom, and the Dominions and Plantations thereunto belonging'. The Navigation Acts reserved colonial trade to British ships and restricted the role of non-British ships in carrying goods to Britain. The development of a network of turnpike roads and the improvement of ports and inland waterways allowed goods to be traded in greater volumes and connected Britain to its empire. Land reclamation, improved crop rotation, selective breeding of livestock and new foods introduced from abroad all contributed to an increase in harvests and the growth of commercial agriculture.

Alongside its economic benefits, trade was also believed to have a civilising effect. In 1755 William Hazeland, a Middlesex schoolteacher, won a prize offered by the University of Cambridge for the best essay on the subject of the mutual support of trade and liberty. According to Hazeland, 'where Trade has flourished', the 'wide experience of men and things which this affords, that active enterprising spirit which it cherishes, those encouragements of genius and invention that are proposed by it, have changed ignorance, barbarity, and inhospitable distrust into mutual confidence, arts and humanity; have given rise to all that is useful and ornamental in human nature'.

In his speech George III pledged that 'the Civil and Religious rights of my loving Subjects are equally dear to Me with the most valuable prerogatives of my Crown'. In Britain civil and religious liberty were believed to be intrinsically linked, a view which paradoxically drew heavily on deeply ingrained anti-Catholic prejudice. In 1688 Parliament had deposed the Catholic James II and in 1689 the Bill of Rights had described his replacement, William of Orange, as he 'whom it hath pleased Almighty God to make the glorious Instrument of Delivering this Kingdome from Popery and Arbitrary Power'. Benjamin Newton, one of the losing

Portrait of King George III
British Library, Egerton 2572, f.24

essayists in the competition described above, drew on popular prejudices about foreigners when he wrote 'now the distinguishing Characteristic of any Nation is invariable … Hence the French-man catches the ostentatious Ambition of his Father; the Spaniard inherits Pride and Sloth; and the Englishman and Hollander naturally succeed to Industry; with this difference, that in the one it produces an open and unreserved Generosity, in the other a sordid and distrustful Avarice'.

George III also proclaimed that 'my Navy is the principal Article of our natural strength' and noted that British victories in the East Indies 'must greatly diminish the Strength and Trade of France in those parts, as well as secure the most solid Benefits to the Commerce and Wealth of my Subjects'. By the mid-eighteenth century the East India Company's role in trade in the Indian Ocean was extensive, covering territories from Africa to China, and it was supported by its own army to maintain order in its colonies and trading stations. Many British investors, manufac-turers and traders had a stake in the company's success. Britain also had extensive trading interests in the Atlantic where, in stark contrast to the theory of trade supporting liberty, the slave trade formed the central part of a triangular trading economy between Europe, West Africa and the Americas. By the middle of the

eighteenth century British ships were responsible for about half of the Atlantic slave trade. Major cities such as London, Liverpool and Bristol were hubs for the trade and many individuals and firms in Britain were recipients of the profits.

Despite the rivalries of competing empires, visits by European ships to the Pacific, the world's largest ocean, were still few and far between. Spain was the predominant European power in the Pacific, but her ships usually followed well-estab-lished routes between existing Spanish territories. The last major British expedition, that of George Anson, which spent much of 1741 and 1742 in the Pacific, was sent during wartime to raid Spanish shipping and settlements. It was devastated by scurvy and stood as a warning of the dangers of sailing the Pacific in the days before accurate charts. Following the end of the Seven Years' War in 1763, rivalry between Britain and France prompted both countries to send expeditions to search for land and commercial opportunities. The British ships of John Byron, Samuel Wallis and Philip Carteret all explored the Pacific in the second half of the 1760s, while the French navigators Louis-Antoine de Bougainville and Jean de Surville led expeditions there in 1768 and 1769 respectively. It was in this context that James Cook's first voyage was planned.

James Cook

James Cook was born in 1728 at Marton in Yorkshire, on the site of present-day Middlesbrough. His father, also called James, had migrated as a young man from southern Scotland to north Yorkshire, where he worked as a farm labourer. James Cook senior married Grace Pace, a local woman, in 1725 and the couple had eight children, only four of whom survived into adulthood. In 1736 he became a farm manager at Great Ayton, a few miles from Marton. James Cook junior attended the village school at Great Ayton where he learned reading, writing and arithmetic, in addition to studying the Bible. In 1745, on the recommendation of Thomas Skottowe, his father's employer, he was taken on as a shop assistant in Staithes, a fishing village on the Yorkshire coast. This brought him into day-to-day contact with the sea and in 1746 he was apprenticed to John Walker, a ship owner in the nearby port of Whitby, to learn the trade of merchant seaman.

Mid-eighteenth-century Whitby was home to a thriving shipbuilding industry, specialising in producing low-cost and robust cargo ships for a growing North Sea trade. Walker owned a fleet of ships that carried coal from Newcastle to London, and during his years working for him Cook rose from apprentice

John Webber,
James Cook, 1776,
oil on canvas
National Portrait Gallery, London

to be master's mate, the second in command of the ship. He learned the art of navigation and gained extensive practical experience of managing ships and their crews on voyages to London and further afield, including the Baltic. In 1755 he was offered the role of master by Walker but turned this down, signing on instead as an able seaman in the Royal Navy. It is not known why Cook made this decision, but against a background of increasing tensions between Britain and France it seems likely that he saw better career opportunities in the Navy.

Cook spent the first two years of the Seven Years' War patrolling the North Atlantic. In 1757 he took part in the capture of the French man-o'-war *Duc d'Aquitaine*, a victory that saw twelve of his shipmates killed and eighty wounded. In 1758 his ship was ordered to Canada as part of a squadron that was to support the campaign against the French. It was here that he learned how to survey and chart coastlines, using these skills to chart parts of the St Lawrence River in preparation for the attack on Quebec in 1759. The British victory at Quebec was the decisive moment in the North American campaign. The next year saw the surrender of French forces at Montreal.

Following the French defeat in Canada, Cook was given responsibility for surveying and charting the rivers and coastlines of Newfoundland, a task he completed methodically between 1762 and 1767. He also developed his skills in astronomy. In August 1766 he observed an eclipse of the Sun from an island off the coast; by comparison with the results of an observation of the same eclipse from Oxford it was possible to establish accurately the longitude of the island. A paper was read at the Royal Society in London summarising the experiment and describing Cook as 'a good mathematician, and very expert in his business'. When, in 1768, the Admiralty and the Royal Society were looking for a mutually acceptable candidate to lead a voyage of exploration and scientific discovery to the Pacific, James Cook's experience made him a suitable candidate.

James Cook,
'A Plan of the Traverse or
Passage from Cape Torment
into the South Channel of
Orleans', 1759
British Library, Add MS 31360, f. 14

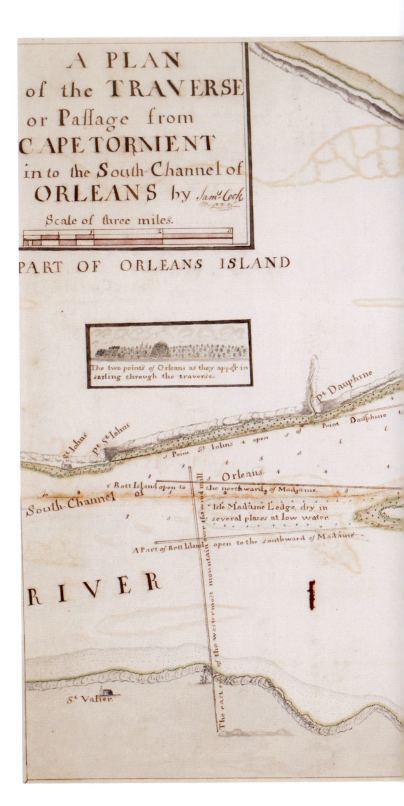

'Cape Torment'

This is one of Cook's charts of the St Lawrence. It shows the
passage from Cap Tourmente (known by the British as 'Cape
Torment') into the channel between the Île d'Orléans and the
shore. The passage was described by the *London Magazine* in 1759
as 'one of the most dangerous parts of the navigation of this [St
Lawrence] river'. The numbers on the chart record the soundings
taken in the passage. It was essential to know the depth of the
water to ensure the safety of the ships. The channel formed the
approach to Quebec. It is not known whether this chart was
drawn in preparation for the British assault on Quebec in 1759
or after the British victory, when Cook was transferred to HMS
Northumberland to continue to chart the St Lawrence River.
Most of the charts that Cook produced were published in the
North American Pilot in 1775 and were used for navigation for
over a century.

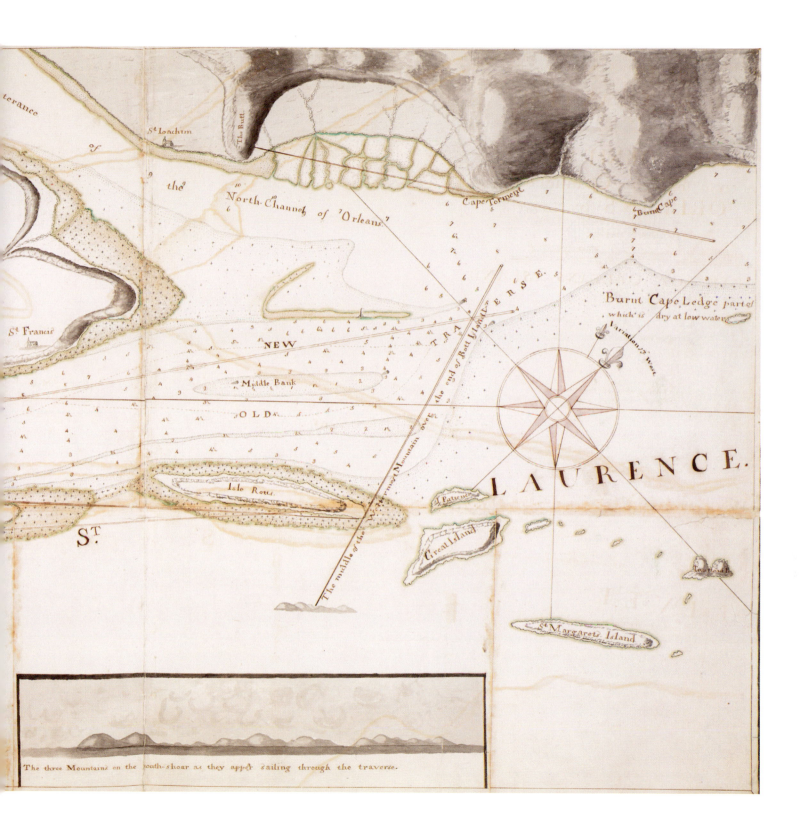

The three Mountains on the south-shoar as they appear sailing through the traverse.

The Royal Society and the European Enlightenment

The Royal Society was founded in 1660 and granted a charter by Charles II in 1662. It was inspired by the ideals of the seventeenth-century Lord Chancellor, Francis Bacon, who argued that observation and experiment, rather than theory or tradition, were the essence of the scientific method. The following decades saw the Society establish itself as Britain's leading scientific and philosophical body. In 1703 Isaac Newton was elected President, an office he held until his death in 1727. Fellows of this period included Robert Boyle, Robert Hooke, Hans Sloane and Christopher Wren. Alexander Pope summarised the spirit of the age when he wrote in response to Newton's death, '*Nature, and Nature's Laws lay hid in Night. God said,* Let Newton Be! *and all was* Light'.

Astronomy and the attempt to understand the universe was one of the core interests of the Royal Society throughout the eighteenth century. In 1716 Edmund Halley, the Astronomer Royal, had published a plan for measuring the distance of the Earth from the Sun by observing the passing of Venus between the two from different points on the Earth's surface. Known as the transit of Venus, this would next occur in 1761 and again in 1769. The observation in 1761 failed due to poor weather and lack of effective co-ordination, leading to calls for the Royal Society to prepare properly for the observation in 1769. With the help of George III, the Society planned to send expeditions to Scandinavia, Canada and the Pacific to record the transit. It was this decision that led to James Cook's first voyage.

The debates of the Royal Society were part of a wider intellectual awakening in eighteenth-century Europe, which has since been known as the Enlightenment. Early Enlightenment science drew on knowledge from outside Europe, including from both the Islamic world and China, where science in the early modern period was more advanced than in Europe. The development of publishing in Europe allowed ideas to move more quickly from one country to another. In England and Wales the abolition in 1695 of the Licensing Act, which had allowed the censorship of publishing by the state, was a symbolic moment in the development of free enquiry. Daily newspapers were established in London for the first time in the early eighteenth century, and as the century progressed there was a growth in the local and regional press. Popular magazines such as *The Gentleman's Magazine* and *The London Magazine* provided another means for ideas to be widely disseminated.

The emphasis on reason as the basis of understanding led to an explosion of works intended to explain or quantify aspects of life. Perhaps the greatest publishing venture of the 'Age of Reason' was *L'Encyclopédie* (The Encyclopaedia), thirty-five volumes of which were published between 1751 and 1780. It was edited by the French philosophers Denis Diderot and Jean Le Rond d'Alembert and contained articles by many of the leading figures of the Enlightenment. Its goal was to provide a rational explanation for all aspects of existence, and it self-consciously sought to supply an alternative to what its authors saw as the superstition and credulity inherent in the teachings of the Catholic Church.

The scope of eighteenth-century science can be seen from a 1761 children's book. Tom Telescope's *The Newtonian System of Philosophy* consists of a comprehensive series of lectures by the eponymous scientist, starting with 'Of MATTER and MOTION', continuing with 'of the UNIVERSE, and particularly of the SOLAR SYSTEM', 'Of the AIR, ATMOSPHERE, and METEORS', 'Of MOUNTAINS, SPRINGS, RIVERS and the SEA', 'Of MINERALS, VEGETABLES and ANIMALS', and concluding with 'Of the five senses of MAN and of his UNDERSTANDING'. Like most eighteenth-century scientists, the fictional child prodigy believed that behind the laws of the universe lay a benign creator: 'As to my part, I am lost in the boundless Abyss. It appears to me that the sun which gives life to the world, is only a beam of the glory of God.'

The idea of science as a complete system of knowledge was

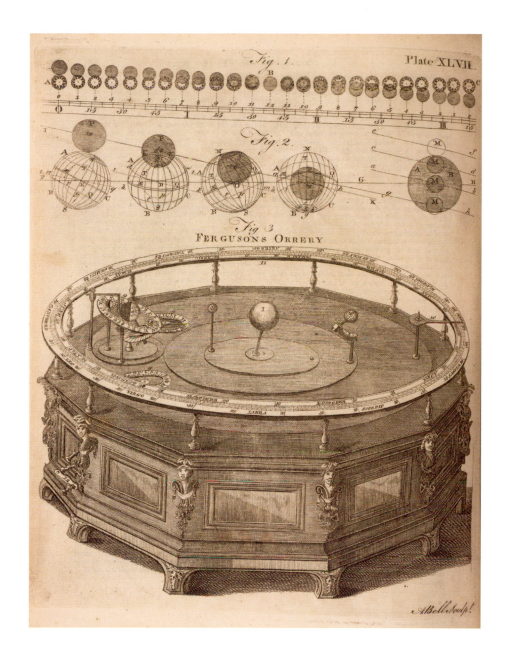

This engraving is from the essay on astronomy in the first edition of the *Encyclopaedia Britannica*. Figure 3 shows James Ferguson's Orrery, a clockwork model of the solar system, with the Sun at the centre and the planets revolving around it.

Encyclopaedia Britannica, 1771, Vol. I, Plate XLVII, facing p. 496
British Library, 738.f.1

central to eighteenth-century intellectual enquiry. The *Encyclopaedia Britannica* was published in Edinburgh in instalments between 1768 and 1771. The introduction to the first complete edition, which appeared in 1771, condemned earlier encyclopaedias, including *L'Encyclopédie,* for 'the folly of attempting to communicate science under the various technical terms arranged in an alphabetical order. Such an attempt is repugnant to the very idea of science'. According to its editors, the *Encyclopaedia Britannica* was different because it 'digested the principles of every science in the form of systems or distinct treatises' so that 'any man of ordinary parts may, if he chuses, learn the principles of Agriculture, of Astronomy, of Botany, of Chemistry, *etc. etc.*'.

Faith in the scientific method led to a belief in progress and modernisation. This was a major philosophical shift, turning on its head the traditional view of modern culture and society as being inferior to that of the 'Golden Age' of classical Greece and Rome. The term 'improvement' was often used as shorthand for the belief that material progress was possible through the practical application of knowledge. The Society for the Encouragement of Arts, Commerce and Manufactures in Great Britain, formed in 1754, epitomised this belief. It sponsored a series of awards for men and women whose work fostered the development of national economic strength. The link between science and commerce was similarly strong in the relationship between the study of the natural world and the development of commercial farming. This is illustrated by the career of Joseph Banks.

Joseph Banks

Joseph Banks's great-grandfather, a successful lawyer, laid the foundations of the family's fortunes, buying a landed estate in south Lincolnshire and establishing himself as a country gentleman. His son married the daughter of a Derbyshire merchant and mine owner, thus considerably enlarging the family's wealth. The couple moved to Revesby Abbey in Lincolnshire in 1714, which became the family seat. In 1741 their son also married a wealthy heiress. By then the family had been established in Lincolnshire for over thirty years and wealth earned or inherited from commerce and industry had been converted into landed property, the basis of entry into the upper echelons of British society. As landowners, the Banks family were involved in the modernisation of agriculture, including the draining of the Fens to create new farmland.

Joseph Banks, who was born in 1743, was the first of his family to be brought up as a member of the upper classes. He was educated at home until the age of nine, when he went to Harrow School. In 1756, at the age of thirteen, he was sent to Eton. Banks failed to distinguish himself as a student at either school. He struggled at Greek and Latin, which formed the basis of the curriculum, and, in the words of one biographer, 'never learnt to spell, nor did he ever master the use of capital letters or punctuation'. But Banks did begin his lifelong enthusiasm for botany at Eton. According to a story he told a friend later in life, this enthusiasm began when walking home one summer evening from swimming in the Thames. Noticing that the sides of the lane 'were richly enamelled with flowers', the thought struck him that 'it is surely more natural that I should be taught to know all these productions of Nature, in preference to Greek and Latin'.

Botany was in fact enjoying huge growth as a public science during this period, and Banks's conversion may have been less spontaneous than he later suggested. In 1735 the Swedish botanist Carl Linnaeus had published his book *Systema Naturae*, which first proposed the scheme for classifying plant life that he was to develop in future works. The Linnaean system assigned each plant to one of twenty-four classes based on its flowers and the number and arrangement of its reproductive organs of stamens and pistils. Each class was subdivided into orders, genera and species. Although Linnaeus's system of classification was later superseded, his method of naming each plant or animal by two words in Latin remains in use today.

In 1764, at the age of twenty-one, Banks established a house in London and set about building a network of friends and collaborators. These included Thomas Pennant, author of *British Zoology* (1766), and Daines Barrington, whose *Naturalist's Journal* (1767) provided a weekly table in which to record observations, including temperature, rainfall and the flowering of plants. In the introduction Barrington expressed the hope that 'from many such journals kept in different parts of the kingdom, perhaps the very best and accurate materials for a General Natural History of Great Britain may in time be expected, as well as many profitable improvements and discoveries in agriculture'.

Sir Joshua Reynolds,
Portrait of Sir Joseph Banks, Bt.,
1771–73, oil on canvas
National Portrait Gallery, London

S. Wale invt et del.

What NATURE *sparing gives, or half denies,*   See in BRITANNIA'S *Lap profusely pours,*
See! *healthfull* INDUSTRY *at large supplies.*   While *heaven-born* SCIENCE *swells th'increasing Stores.*

Ecce! ferunt Pueri Calathis Tibi Lilia plenis.   VIRG.

J. Miller Sculp.

Philip Miller, *The Gardener's Dictionary*, 8th edition, 1768. Frontispiece.
British Library, 33.i.4–5

Philip Miller, another of Banks's friends, was the author of *The Gardener's Dictionary*, a two-volume work which rivalled the *Encyclopaedia Britannica* in scale and ambition in its chosen field. The eighth edition, published in 1768, adopted the Linnaean system of classification and did much to popularise it as 'the latest system of Botany'. Miller was gardener to the Worshipful Company of Apothecaries and superintendent of its botanic garden at Chelsea, which provided a source of ingredients for new medicines. The engraving opposite his title page illustrates how the application of new knowledge to the improvement of agriculture was often set in a patriotic context. Amid Arcadian scenes of nature's bounty, Britannia's shield and spear sit under the tree, reinforcing the message of the poem below:

What NATURE sparing gives, or half denies,
See! Healthful INDUSTRY at large supplies.
See! In BRITANNIA's lap profusely pours,
While heaven-born SCIENCE swells increasing stores.

Collecting of specimens was also important to the study of the natural world. In 1766 Banks embarked on an overseas collecting trip to Newfoundland. On his return he began the work of

This plate shows the 24 classes of plant in the Linnaean system. It is from Joseph Banks's copy of *An introduction to botany containing an explanation of the theory of that science, and an interpretation of its technical terms, extracted from the works of Linnæus*, by James Lee, 1760. British Library, 450.f.4

cataloguing the specimens, helped by Daniel Solander, a Swede who had studied under Linnaeus at Uppsala University and who was responsible for the natural history collections of the recently opened British Museum. Fanny Burney described Solander as 'very sociable, full of talk, information and entertainment'. Banks also employed artists, including Sydney Parkinson, a young man from Edinburgh, to draw the plants in preparation for a projected publication.

On hearing of the Royal Society's plans to send a ship to the Pacific to observe the transit of Venus, Banks offered part of the funding in return for berths aboard for himself and his party,

including Solander, Parkinson and Alexander Buchan, another young artist from Scotland. Banks's role in the voyage would establish him as a central figure in British science. As President of the Royal Society from 1778 to 1820 he would be a key proponent of the transplantation of new crops and farming techniques across the British Empire. As the leading advocate for the establishment of a British prison colony at Botany Bay, he would prove critical to the British colonisation of Australia and later other parts of the Pacific.

THE FIRST VOYAGE

1768–71

The Instructions

Until James Cook's voyages, the South Pacific was primarily an imagined space to Europeans. Since the time of ancient Greece there had been a belief that a Southern Continent existed that matched in size the great northern landmasses. Ptolemy, who is regarded as the founder of Western cartography, suggested its existence in the second century CE and it subsequently appeared in many European maps. A theory developed that, in order to balance the world as it spun on its axis, there had to be a landmass equivalent to Asia in the south. Early mapping of the Americas seemed to support this belief by showing two seemingly equivalent landmasses in the north and south.

In 1767 the British cartographer Alexander Dalrymple published *An Account of the Discoveries made in the South Pacifick Ocean*, which argued, from fleeting sightings of land by navigators, that there was an extensive landmass awaiting discovery in the Pacific. He wrote: 'We have traces from antient times, warranted by latter experience, of rich and valuable countries in it; no subject can be more interesting, to a commercial state, than the discovery of new countries and people, to invigorate the hand of industry, by opening new vents for manufactures'. He also argued that 'from a consideration of the weight of land to water, that a Continent is wanting on the South of the Equator, to counterpoize the land on the North, and to maintain the equilibrium necessary for the Earth's motion'.

This map shows the outline of Australia, or 'New Holland', as known in Europe at the time the *Endeavour* sailed. Further down the page are parts of the coast of Tasmania (centre) and New Zealand (right), both fleetingly visited by Abel Tasman in the 1640s, but otherwise unknown in Europe.

The Klenke Atlas, Amsterdam, 1658
British Library, Maps K.A.R. (5.)

In April 1768 Cook was appointed to lead the joint Admiralty–Royal Society expedition to the Pacific to observe the transit of Venus. His skills as both cartographer and astronomer were crucial to his selection and it was probably also significant that the ship chosen for the voyage was a former Whitby collier, recently renamed the *Endeavour*. His orders, jointly agreed between the Admiralty and the Royal Society, instructed him to sail to Tahiti via Cape Horn, 'using your best endeavours to arrive there at least a Month or six Weeks before' to allow time to prepare for the observation. Tahiti was a last-minute choice, following the return of a British expedition led by Samuel Wallis in April 1768 with news of the first European landing at the island.

On leaving Tahiti, Cook was to follow a second set of orders, which came in a sealed packet and were from the Admiralty only. These instructed him to search for new lands, including the Southern Continent, the discovery of which 'will redound greatly to the Honour of this Nation as a Maritime Power, as well as to the Dignity of the Crown of Great Britain, and may tend greatly to the advancement of the Trade and Navigation thereof'. If land was found he was to survey the coastline and 'observe the Nature of the Soil, and the Products thereof; the Beasts and Fowls that inhabit or frequent it, the fishes that are to be found'. The orders also noted 'in case you find any Mines, Minerals or valuable stones you are to bring home Specimens of each, as also such Species of the Seeds of the Trees, Fruits and Grains as you may be able to collect'.

The Admiralty also gave instructions on how to manage relationships with the inhabitants of the places the *Endeavour* visited. These may have been prompted by news of Samuel Wallis's actions in Tahiti. According to Wallis, his ship had been subject to a determined attack by a fleet of canoes while at anchor and to repel this he had fired several broadsides, killing many of his attackers. He had also turned his cannons on crowds watching from the shore, killing more people, before landing and claiming the island for Britain by conquest. As with many other such incidents, no detailed contemporary accounts of the conflict survive from the Tahitian perspective.

The Admiralty instructed Cook:

> *to observe the Genius, Temper, Disposition and Number of the Natives, if there be any, and endeavour by all proper means to cultivate a Friendship and Alliance with them, making them Presents of such Trifles as they may Value, inviting them to Traffick, and Shewing them every kind of Civility and Regard; taking Care however not to suffer yourself to be surprized by them, but to be always upon your guard against any Accident.*

In regard to lands previously unvisited by Europeans, the Admiralty instructed 'you are also with the Consent of the Natives to take possession of Convenient Situations in the Country in the name of the King of Great Britain'.

Cook also received written advice from Lord Morton, President of the Royal Society and one of the commissioners of the Board of Longitude. Morton urged Cook to 'restrain the wanton use of Fire Arms' and to keep in mind:

> *that shedding the blood of those people is a crime of the highest nature ... They are the natural, and in the strictest sense of the word, the legal possessors of the several Regions they inhabit. No European Nation has a right to occupy any part of their country, or settle among them without their voluntary consent. Conquest over such people can give no just title; because they could never be the Agressors.*

Morton's concerns reflected both an Enlightenment disavowal of the earlier legacy of European conquest and settlement abroad and a patriotic view that exploration informed by the British values of liberty and the promotion of trade would be conducted differently. The actions of the Spanish *conquistadors* in South America were often cited as an example of the ruthless behaviour of other nations. Johann Forster, the naturalist on Cook's second voyage, expressed this view when he wrote, 'The Spaniards were cruel in a less refined age; we should, with more light & principles, endeavour to avoid the reproach of following in their footsteps'.

Despite such good intentions, Cook's instructions from both the Admiralty and Lord Morton contain substantial ambiguities. What are the 'proper means' to cultivate friendships and alliances with people unfamiliar with European laws and customs, and what means are improper? How simple is it to distinguish 'self-defence' from the 'wanton use of firearms' when landing in unfamiliar places without any knowledge of local power structures or social conventions? In the absence of shared language, laws and economic systems, is it possible to 'take possession' of land with the 'voluntary consent' of the people who live there?

The Atlantic

The *Endeavour* sailed from Plymouth on 26 August 1768. The waters of the North Atlantic were well known to British sailors and the first few pages of Cook's journal are uneventful. By contrast, the early entries in Joseph Banks's journal are alive with a sense of excitement. The sea that Cook knew as familiar and unremarkable was to Banks the home of myriad creatures, many not yet classified or described by science. On 4 September he noted that an insect caught that day:

> *was possest of more beautiful Colouring than any thing in nature I have ever seen, hardly excepting gems […] This which we called opalinum shone in the water with all the splendor and variety of colours that we observe in a real opal; he livd in the Glass of salt water in which he was put for examination several hours; darting about with great agility, and at every motion shewing an almost infinite variety of changeable colours.*

The collecting of marine creatures would continue throughout the voyage and a number of these specimens still exist in museum collections today. This example of the jaw of a large squid is believed to have been collected by Banks on 3 March 1769, soon after the *Endeavour* entered the Pacific. He wrote of it in his journal: 'I found also this day a large Sepia cuttle fish laying on the water just dead but so pull'd to peices by the birds that his Species could not be determin'd; only this I know that of him was made one of the best soups I ever eat.'

The *Endeavour* stopped at the Portuguese island of Madeira for five days in mid-September, providing the first opportunity for Banks and Solander to collect specimens on land. They were helped by Thomas Heberden, the British chief physician of the island, a keen natural philosopher. Banks cast a critical eye over the 'simple and unimproved' nature of the island's industries and, with the superiority of an eighteenth-century Englishman

Specimen of the mouthparts of a large squid.
Royal College of Surgeons, London

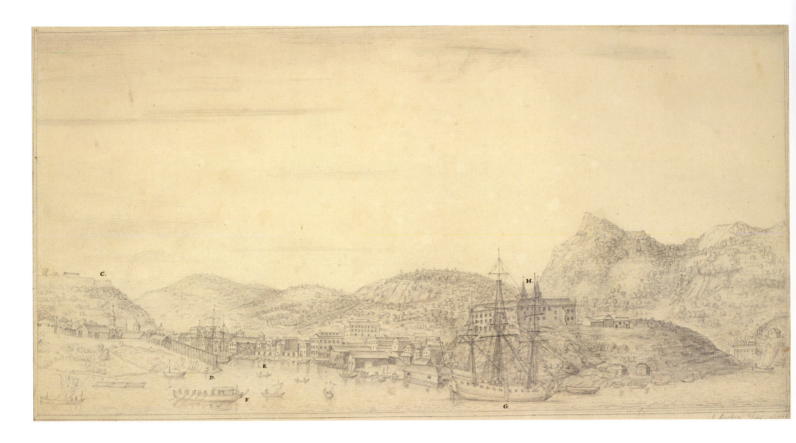

This is one of three sections of a panoramic drawing. The letters provide a key to places of interest.

Alexander Buchan, 'A View of the Town of Rio de Janeiro from the Anchoring-Place', 1769
British Library, Add MS 23920, f. 8

abroad, dismissed the Portuguese as 'far behind all the rest of Europe, except possibly the Spaniards'. Nonetheless he acknowledged that 'the climate is so fine that any man might wish it was in his power to live here under the benefits of English laws and liberties'.

The ship crossed the equator on 26 October. In line with naval tradition, the crew organised a ceremonial ducking in the ocean for those who had not been to the southern hemisphere before. Banks commented, 'Captn Cooke and Doctor Solander were on the Black list, as were my self my servants and doggs, which I was obliged to compound for by giving the Duckers a certain quantity of Brandy for which they willingly excused us the ceremony'.

At Rio de Janeiro, the centre of the Portuguese empire in South America, the expedition was refused permission to land,

except to collect provisions under military escort. Cook wrote of his interview with the Viceroy: 'He certainly did not believe a word about our being bound to the Southward to Observe the transit of Venus but look'd upon it only as an invented story to cover some other design we must be upon'. Banks secretly landed for a single day, and found himself tantalised by a country which 'abounded with vast variety of plants and animals, mostly such as have not been described by our naturalists'. He attributed the Portuguese secrecy to a desire to conceal the location of rich gold and diamond mines, which he nonetheless sought to discover. He recorded that these 'are situated far up in the countrey, indeed no one could tell me how far … for everybody who is found on the road without being able to give a good account of himself is hangd immediately'.

Tierra del Fuego

Introduction

After leaving Rio the ship continued towards the tip of South America. January is midsummer in the southern hemisphere but nonetheless the cold prompted Cook to issue winter clothing, known as 'fearnought jackets', to the crew. On 11 January 1769 Tierra del Fuego, an archipelago at the tip of South America, was sighted. Its name, meaning 'land of fire', was given by Ferdinand Magellan in 1520 on passing through the strait (now called the Strait of Magellan) between it and mainland South America and observing fires made by the inhabitants. The seas around Tierra del Fuego are treacherous and it was not until 1616 that the Dutch navigator Jacob Le Maire passed to the south of it. Le Maire's expedition was funded by the merchants of the Dutch town of Hoorn and on passing the southern tip of South America he gave it the name Cape Hoorn.

Before rounding the Cape, the *Endeavour* anchored to take on wood and water and a camp was established on shore. Although the Spanish and Portuguese empires controlled much of South America, the south of the continent remained uncolonised and, from a European perspective, largely unexplored. This was the first time the expedition encountered non-European peoples who were not living under European colonial government. Following Columbus's mistaken assumption that he had reached Asia in 1492, the inhabitants of the Americas had become known by Europeans as 'Indians', a term that would be regularly applied in the Pacific. Banks wrote:

before we had walkd 100 yards many Indians made their appearance on the other side of the bay … but on seeing our numbers to be ten or twelve they retreated. Dr Solander and myself then walkd forward 100 yards before the rest and two of the Indians advanc'd also and set themselves down about 50 yards from their companions. As soon as we came up they rose and each of them threw a stick he had in his hand away from him and us, a token no doubt of peace, they then

walkd briskly towards the other party and wavd to us to follow, which we did and were received with many uncouth signs of freindship.

The men they met are believed to have been members of the Haush people, who lived in the area at the time. The formalised nature of the meeting on the beach suggests that a means of establishing peaceful relations with foreign visitors had been instituted. During their visit the party observed a wide range of European goods including 'Sail Cloth, Brown woollen Cloth, Beads, nails, Glass &c' and also distributed presents themselves. Three men came on board ship and Banks noted that they were familiar with the use of guns, 'making signs to me to shoot a seal who was following us in the boat'.

In the eighteenth century Tierra del Fuego was the most southerly land inhabited by humans. The *Endeavour* stopped there for five days and during that time Banks collected as much information about the place and its people as he could. Working to his instructions, the artist Alexander Buchan drew a series of pictures of people, houses and artefacts. These show the Haush people and their culture at a time before the depopulation of the region, caused by disease and conflict in the late nineteenth century. They also illustrate the process of ethnographic collecting and documentation that Banks would follow during the voyage. For Banks, the goal of accurately recording the societies he visited ran alongside his wish to collect materials with which to establish his reputation in intellectual circles at home. In recording non-European societies and cultures, Banks and his party brought their own assumptions with them, and their paintings and journal accounts are influenced by the conventions of European art and philosophy.

Almost nothing is known about the life of Alexander Buchan before he joined the voyage. At Tierra del Fuego Banks described how Buchan suffered an epileptic seizure during a journey

inland to collect plants. He later died in Tahiti on 17 April 1769 following another epileptic seizure. Banks wrote after attending his funeral:

> *I sincerely regret him as an ingenious and good young man, but his Loss to me is irretrevable, my airy dreams of entertaining my freinds in England with the scenes that I am to see here are vanishd. No account of the figures and dresses of men can be satisfactory unless illustrated with figures: had providence spard him a month longer what an advantage would it have been to my undertaking but I must submit.*

Buchan's paintings from Tierra del Fuego are his main surviving legacy. As the above passage makes clear, they were intended to be published in Banks's account of the voyage. They therefore relate closely to passages in Banks's journal describing the people and customs of the region.

Alexander Buchan,
'A View of the *Endeavour*'s
Watering Place in the Bay
of Good Success', 1769
British Library, Add MS 23920, f. 11

A Man and Woman of Tierra del Fuego

Banks wrote of the men he met in Tierra del Fuego: 'Their Cloaths are no more than a kind of cloak of Guanicoe or seal skin thrown loose over their shoulders and reaching down nearly to their knees … a few of them had shoes of raw seal hide … they have a kind of wreath of brown worsted which they wear over their Foreheads'. He described watching the women, who were dressed in similar fashion, collecting shellfish 'at low water with a basket in one hand, a stick with a point and barb in the other, and a satchel on their backs which they filld with shellfish'.

Alexander Buchan, 'A Man of the Island of Tierra del Fuego' and 'A Woman of the Island of Tierra del Fuego', 1769
British Library, Add MS 23920, f. 16 and f. 17

A Family of Tierra del Fuego

In his journal Banks described a village he visited about two miles from the landing site at the Bay of Good Success on 20 January 1769:

> *It consisted of not more than twelve or fourteen huts or wigwams of the most unartificial construction imaginable, indeed no thing bearing the name of a hut could possibly be built with less trouble. They consisted of a few poles set up and meeting together at the top in a conical figure, these were coverd on the weather side with a few boughs and a little grass, on the lee side about one eighth part of the circle was left open and against this opening was a fire made.*

Alexander Buchan,
'Inhabitants of the Island of
Terra del Fuego in their Hut', 1769
British Library, Add MS 23920, f. 14a

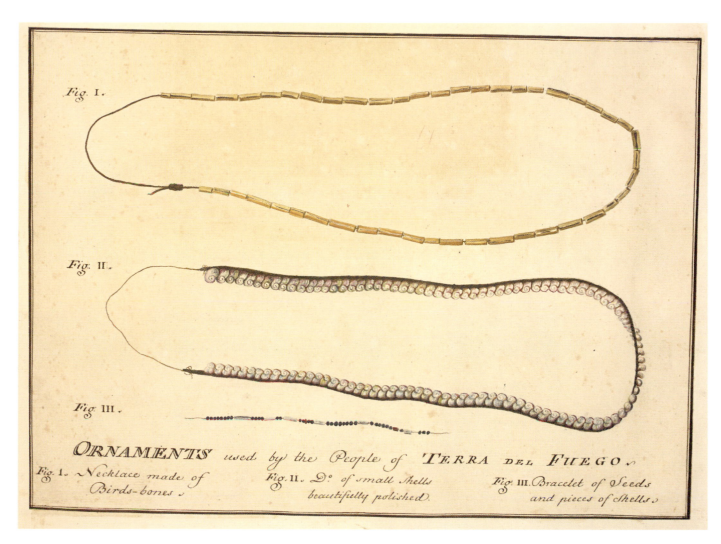

Fig. I.

Fig. II.

Fig. III.

ORNAMENTS *used by the People of* TERRA DEL FUEGO.

Fig. I. Necklace made of Birds-bones.   *Fig. II. D° of small Shells beautifully polished.*   *Fig. III. Bracelet of Seeds and pieces of Shells.*

Artefacts

Buchan also drew artefacts collected by Banks and his party, including this group of necklaces. Numbers and captions have been added to the drawing for each necklace, and these would have been copied by the engraver in the published version of the drawings. A necklace collected on Cook's voyages survives in the collections of the Cambridge Museum of Archaeology and Anthropology. Because Cook also called at Tierra del Fuego on his second voyage, it is not certain on which voyage this was collected, although it is similar to the second necklace in Buchan's drawing.

above
Alexander Buchan,
'Ornaments used by the
People of Terra del Fuego', 1769
British Library, Add MS 23920, f. 20b

right
Shell necklace,
Tierra del Fuego
Museum of Archaeology and
Anthropology, Cambridge

Tahiti

Sydney Parkinson, 'House and
Plantation of a Chief of the Island
of Otaheite', 1770
British Library, Add MS 23921, f. 10b

Introduction

On the journey from Cape Horn to Tahiti the expedition found only empty seas in uncharted areas that some European cartographers had believed were part of the Great Southern Continent. Banks noted with satisfaction 'the number of square degrees of their land which we have already changed into water'. In early April the ship began to pass groups of small islands and on 13 April 1769 it arrived at Tahiti, anchoring, like Wallis, in Matavai Bay. Since the departure of Wallis, Tahiti had been visited by a French expedition led by Louis Antoine de Bougainville. Bougainville's later account of the sexual liaisons of his men, and his naming of Tahiti as the 'new Cythera' after the island near which Aphrodite, the Greek goddess of love, emerged from the sea, would play an important part in establishing the European stereotype of Tahiti as a place of sexual freedom. A consequence of the British and French visits was the arrival of venereal disease, which had not been present before.

As the *Endeavour* approached shore, canoes came out with food to trade. Cook led a party ashore, where the Tahitians encouraged each visitor to follow their example and gather a green bough, which was then dropped in a cleared patch of ground to establish peace. Banks enthused: 'The scene we saw was the truest picture of an arcadia of which we were going to be kings than the imagination can form'. More practically, Cook's first priority was to make contact with the island's ruler or rulers and thereby to gain supplies and permission to establish a camp on shore. During Wallis's visit good relations had been established with a leading woman, called Purea, who was mistakenly identified as the 'Queen of Otaheite'. On going ashore John Gore, who had sailed with Wallis, told Cook that 'a very great revolution must have happen'd – not near the number of inhabitants [and] a great number of houses raiz'd'.

The political situation on the island had, indeed, changed dramatically since Wallis's visit, driven by the question of dynastic succession to the role of paramount chief or *ari'i rahi*. Purea and her husband, Amo, had been foiled in their ambition to establish their son in this role, and were defeated in a bloody battle by a combination of their enemies. These included Tuteha, who visited Matavai Bay soon after the *Endeavour*'s arrival. Cook exchanged names with him, which was a means of forming alliances in Tahitian society. Purea arrived in Matavai Bay accompanied by a fleet of canoes on 28 April. Robert Molyneux, the ship's master, who had sailed with Wallis, pointed her out to Banks:

> *Our attention was now intirely diverted from every other object to the examination of a personage we had heard so much spoken of in Europe: she appeared to be about 40, tall and very lusty, her skin white and her eyes full of meaning, she might have been hansome when young but now few or no traces of it were left.*

Cook noted that, although she was chief of her own 'family or tribe', Purea 'hath no authority over the rest of the Inhabitants' and instead Tuteha 'is to all appearances the Chief man of the Island'. Tuteha had visited the *Endeavour* regularly since its arrival, bringing supplies with him. Cook wrote that he 'did not appear very well pleased at the Notice we took of Obariea [Purea] but I soon put him into a good humor by takeing him on board and makeing him some presents'.

Like earlier European visitors, many of the British sought sex with Tahitian women. Banks wrote with enthusiasm of an early visit ashore when 'I espied among the common crowd a very pretty girl with a fire in her eyes'. Although many sensationalist

accounts were later to circulate about the sexual conquests of Banks and others at Tahiti, the existing journal accounts suggest that most of the men sought stable relationships with individual women, who often sought European goods in return. (Cook, who seems to have remained celibate throughout the voyages, was an exception.) Banks was thwarted in the above encounter by a combination of the jealous wife of a local chief and the timely disappearance of Solander's snuff box and a set of opera glasses. A few days later he was writing of his relationship with one of Purea's retinue, a young woman he called Otheothea.

The attraction of European goods as trading commodities was such that during the visit pilfering from the ship and onshore camp by both sailors and Tahitians was common. Such thefts would recur over all three voyages in most of the places visited and were the most common source of disputes between ship and shore. The most serious incident during the stay at Tahiti happened when a man snatched a musket from one of the marines. Cook, Banks and others were away from the landing site and returned to find that the midshipman in charge had allowed the marines to fire at the fleeing man, killing him and probably injuring others. In a scene that would be replayed following other confrontations in other places, Banks described how an old man acted as an intermediary:

Before night by his means we got together a few of them and explaining to them that the man who sufferd was guilty of a crime deserving of death (for so we were forcd to make it) we retird to the ship not well pleasd with the days expedition, guilty no doubt in some measure of the death of a man who the most severe laws of equity would not have condemnd to so severe a punishment.

Following Morton's advice, Cook's determination to avoid the 'wanton use of firearms' led him to seek other means of bringing about the return of missing property. In early May the astronomical quadrant, which was essential to observing the transit of Venus, disappeared. Cook recorded his actions in his journal. 'Immediately a resolution was taken to detain all the large Canoes that were in the Bay, and to seize upon Tootaha [Tuteha] and some others of the Principle people, and keep them in Custody until the Quadrant was produce'd.'

This was the first occasion on which Cook took hostages in order to recover a missing item, a tactic he would use regularly in the future and which would lead to his death in Hawai'i. On this occasion the quadrant was soon returned, but it took several days for Cook and Tuteha to be reconciled and during this time the islanders stopped bringing provisions to trade. The reconciliation involved an exchange of gifts and was marked by a large gathering and a public display of wrestling.

This Gregorian reflecting telescope, made by James Short *c*. 1758, is similar to those used by Cook's party to observe the transit of Venus.
Whipple Museum of the History of Science, Cambridge

opposite
These drawings of Fort Venus are by Charles Praval, who joined the *Endeavour* on the voyage home, and are believed to be later copies of originals that no longer survive.
British Library, Add MS 7085, f. 8

The Transit of Venus

The passage of Venus between the Earth and the Sun, known as the transit of Venus, occurs twice in quick succession with more than a century between each pair of transits. Following the failure of the observation in 1761, the transit in 1769 was the last opportunity until 1874 to gain accurate observations. Edmund Halley had argued that by using parallax, the difference in angle when viewing an object from different locations, it would be possible to calculate the distance of the Earth from the Sun. In 1619 Johannes Kepler had established a formula for calculating the relative distance of each planet from the Sun. If the actual distance of the Earth from the Sun was known then the size of the solar system could also be calculated.

The *Endeavour* had arrived at Tahiti about six weeks before the transit of Venus. Cook 'therefore, without delay, resolved to pitch upon some spot upon the North-East point of the Bay, properly situated for observing the Transit of Venus, and at the same time under the command of the Ship's Guns, and there to throw up a small fort for our defence'. He attempted to explain the purpose of the fort to the Tahitians. 'Whether they understood us or no is uncertain, but no one appear'd the least displeased at what we was about. Indeed the Ground we had fixed upon was of no use to them, being part of the sandy Beach upon the shore of the Bay.'

Cook observed the transit at 'Fort Venus' with Charles Green and Solander. He also sent parties to the northeast coast and to the nearby island of Mo'orea. Banks, who was one of the party on Mo'orea, described how he explained the observation to the local people: 'After the first Internal contact was over I went to my Companions at the observatory carrying with me Tarroa, Nuna and some of their cheif atendants; to them we shewd the planet

upon the sun and made them understand that we came on purpose to see it.' The islanders who looked through the telescope that day may have perceived the observation as a type of religious ceremony conducted by the visitors. Venus was known in the Society Islands as Ta'urua-nui, the daughter of Atea, the mother of the stars, and was a sign of peace and prosperity.

The transit was observed with reflecting telescopes, which use a mirror to focus light. The aim was to record accurate timings for each of four phases of the planet's journey across the face of the Sun. Cook wrote of the observation from Fort Venus:

> *Not a Clowd was to be seen the whole day, and the Air was perfectly clear, so that we had every advantage we could desire … We very distinctly saw an Atmosphere or dusky shade round the body of the Planet, which very much disturbed the times of the Contacts, particularly the two internal ones. Dr. Solander observed as well as Mr. Green and my self, and we differ'd from one another in observing the times of the Contacts much more than could be expected.*

The same problem occurred at the observations in Norway and Canada and we now know that this was caused by turbulence in the Earth's atmosphere blurring the image of Venus in the telescope (known as the 'black drop effect'). Despite this, the French astronomer Jérôme Lalande was able to use the data gathered in 1761 and 1769 to calculate the distance from Earth to Sun as 153 million kilometres, an error of less than three percent from the actual distance of 149.6 million kilometres (92.9 million miles).

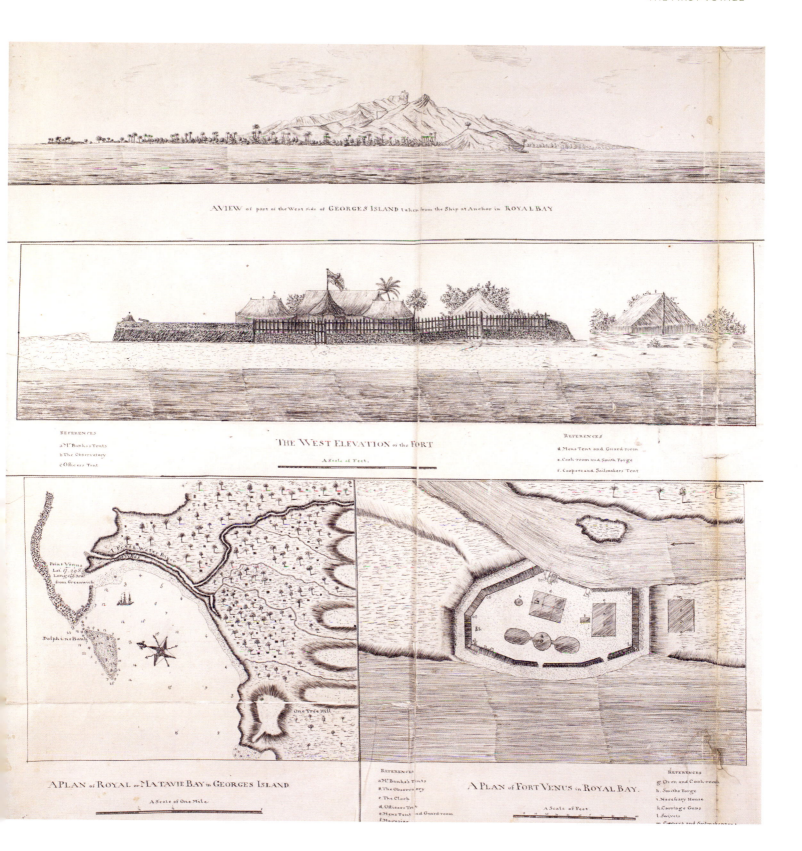

A VIEW of part of the West side of GEORGES ISLAND taken from the Ship at Anchor in ROYAL BAY.

REFERENCES

a Mr Banks's Tents
b The Observatory
c Officers Tent

THE WEST ELEVATION of the FORT

A Scale of Feet.

REFERENCES

d Mens Tent and Guard-room
e Cook-room and Smith Forge
f Coopers and Sailmakers Tent

A PLAN of ROYAL or MATAVIE BAY in GEORGES ISLAND

A Scale of One Mile

REFERENCES

a Mr Banks's Tents
b The Observatory
c The Clock
d Officers Tent
e Mens Tent and Guard-room
f Magazine

A PLAN of FORT VENUS in ROYAL BAY.

A Scale of Feet

REFERENCES

g Oven and Cook-room
h Smiths Forge
i Necessary House
k Carriage Guns
l Swivels
m Coopers and Sailmakers t

Sydney Parkinson

left
Sydney Parkinson,
Self-Portrait, oil on canvas
Natural History Museum, London

opposite, above
Sydney Parkinson,
[A View in Tahiti with Taro, Yams
and Breadfruit Tree], 1769
British Library, Add MS 23921, f. 9

opposite, below
Sydney Parkinson,
'Vessels of the Island of Otaha',
1769
British Library, Add MS 23921, f. 17

Sydney Parkinson was born in Edinburgh in about 1745 to Elizabeth and Joel Parkinson. The family were Quakers, and despite his father's early death Parkinson had a good education and was apprenticed as a woollen draper. His talent as a natural history artist quickly became apparent and, based on the style of his surviving work, it is thought that he studied under William de la Cour, who had opened a publicly funded art school in Edinburgh in 1760.

Parkinson exhibited a number of his flower paintings at the Free Society of Artists in London in 1765. Following this he was employed by James Lee to draw plants in his Hammersmith nursery and to teach painting to his daughter Ann. It was through Lee that Parkinson received commissions from Banks to paint specimens from his expedition to Newfoundland and Labrador, and to make copies for him of drawings of Indian mammals and birds. Following this, he was recruited by Banks as the draughtsman for the *Endeavour* voyage, to draw plant and animal specimens collected in the Pacific.

During the voyage Parkinson made over 1,300 drawings. Banks recorded in his journal in Australia 'in 14 days just, one draughtsman has made 94 sketch drawings, so quick a hand has he acquird by use'. To complete the work quickly and to conserve scarce paints Parkinson would often create a sketch of a plant and add in sample colours for each of the elements depicted, so that the full version could be worked up when he returned home.

After Buchan died, Parkinson also took on responsibility for drawing landscapes and portraits. Owing to the shortage of paints he used pen and wash instead and his drawings have a distinctively recognisable quality. The two drawings here show different aspects of life in Tahiti and the neighbouring islands. Breadfruit was one of the staple crops of the islands and the belief that 'bread' literally grew on trees contributed significantly to the European stereotype of Tahiti as a paradise island. The second picture shows a double sailing canoe of Taha'a, one of the outlying islands. Both drawings were probably intended to form the basis of engravings in the published account of the voyage.

Parkinson died on the return voyage in January 1771. His natural history drawings were completed in England and copper plates were made from them. However, the scale of the project led to delays and the book Banks intended to publish was never completed. It was not until the 1980s that a Natural History Museum project published 738 engravings in a thirty-four-part volume entitled *Banks' Florilegium*. Many of Parkinson's depictions of people and landscapes have become iconic images in their own right.

Tupaia

When Purea visited Matavai Bay she was often accompanied by a man called Tupaia, who acted as her advisor. Tupaia was a high priest or *tuhuna* of Oro, the god of war, whose main temple was at Taputapuatea on his home island of Ra'iatea, and also a member of the *arioi*, a cult group distinguished by particular tattoos. As well as officiating in religious ceremonies, priests acted as custodians of knowledge, including medicine, astronomy and navigation. During the stay at Tahiti, Tupaia became close to Banks, acting as an advisor and guide and effectively becoming one of the scientific party. Cook described him as 'a very intelligent person and to know more of the Geography of the Islands situated in these seas, their produce and the religion laws and customs of the inhabitants than any one we had met with'. The journals of both Banks and Cook include long descriptions of Tahitian society and customs, which are believed to be based on conversations with Tupaia.

When the *Endeavour* was ready to leave Tahiti, Tupaia and his servant Taiato, a boy of ten or twelve years of age, joined the voyage with the intention of travelling to Britain. At the island of Huahine, Tupaia acted as both interpreter and intermediary, ensuring that the new arrivals observed the correct social and religious norms. Under his guidance William Monkhouse, the surgeon, took part in the welcoming ritual as the nearest British equivalent of a priest and healer in Polynesian society. The *Endeavour* arrived at Ra'iatea, Tupaia's home island, in late July 1769. Tupaia had left Ra'iatea following its conquest by men from the island of Bora Bora, led by their chief Puni. One of his motives in allying with the British seems to have been the hope that the *Endeavour*'s guns could be used to help oust the invaders. Parkinson's journal records Tupaia's history of the conflict:

> The chiefs of Otaheite, and the neighbouring islands, banished such of their criminals as were convicted of thefts, and other crimes which they thought did not deserve death, to an adjacent island called Bolobola ... Opoone, who was one of the worst of these criminals, by artful insinuations so wrought on the rest, that he was admitted their chief, or king; and, growing still more powerful, by frequent acquisitions of prisoners, he adventured to make war on the people of Otahaw ... He afterwards conquered Yoolee-etea, and other islands.

Tupaia sailed on the *Endeavour* to New Zealand and Australia. He died at Batavia (modern-day Jakarta) on the return journey, after catching a fever. In the 1990s, the discovery of a copy of a letter written by Banks to Dawson Turner, a fellow member of the Royal Society, describing Tupaia drawing a picture in New Zealand, led to the attribution of a group of drawings to him. These had been unattributed, but were believed to be by the same person owing to similarities in style, including in the hair, hands and feet of the people pictured. It had previously been suggested that they were by Banks, because of apparent connections to passages in his journal.

No picture of Tupaia is known to survive. This faint drawing of two women dancing is one of the series attributed to him following the discovery of Banks's letter to Dawson Turner.
Tupaia, [Two Girls holding Fans or Rattles], 1769
British Library, Add MS 15508, f. 13

The Chief Mourner and a Dancing Girl

The drawing on the right shows the costume of the Chief Mourner, who officiated at Tahitian funeral ceremonies. Each part of his sacred regalia had a different symbolism and when dressed he had the power to 'galvanise' the gods in order to help the deceased into *Rohutu-no'ano'a*, the *arioi*'s paradise. On 10 June 1769 Banks asked his friend Tubourai if he could take part in a funeral procession. He later wrote:

> He put on his dress, most Fantastical tho not unbecoming, the figure annexd will explain it far better than words can. I was next prepard by stripping off my European cloths and putting me on a small strip of cloth round my waist, the only garment I was allowd to have, but I had no pretensions to be ashamd of my nakedness for neither of the women were a bit more coverd than myself. They then began to smut me and themselves with charcoal and water, the Indian boy was compleatly black, the women and myself as low as our shoulders. We then set out ...

The procession passed the fort 'to the surprize of our freinds' and then continued along the shore as people in its path fled, 'running to the first shelter, hiding themselves under grass or whatever else would contain them'. After the ceremony Banks wrote that 'we went into the river and scrubbd one another till it was dark before the blacking would come off'.

The drawing on the left shows a dancing girl. Banks's journal records a number of dances at Tahiti and nearby islands and it is not known when the drawing was made. Banks records that at Ra'iatea on 7 August 1769 he 'took Mr Parkinson to the Heiva that he might scetch the dresses' and it is possible that Tupaia accompanied him. In the image the dancing girl is shown with her mouth distorted. Banks described how the dancers he witnessed set 'their mouths askew in the most extraordinary manner'. He also described the style of dancing in his journal:

> In this dress they advancd sideways keeping excellent time to the drums which beat brisk and loud; they soon began to shake their hips giving the folds of cloth that lay upon them a very quick motion which was continued during the whole dance, they sometimes standing, sometimes sitting and sometimes resting on their knees and elbows and generaly moving their fingers with a quickness scarce to be imagind.

Tupaia, [Dancing girl and Chief Mourner], 1769
British Library, Add MS 15508, f. 9

Tupaia,
[Musicians of Tahiti], 1769
British Library, Add MS 15508, f. 11

A Group of Musicians

This watercolour depicts four *arioi* musicians, including two nose flute players and two drummers. The latter are dressed in the *tiputa*, a poncho made from undyed bark cloth. Banks described this or a similar group in his journal on 12 June 1769:

> There was a large concourse of people round this band, which consisted of 2 flutes and three drums, the drummers acompanying their musick with their voices; they sang many songs generaly in praise of us, for these gentlemen like Homer of old must be poets as well as musicians. The Indians seeing us entertaind with their musick, asked us to sing them an English song, which we most readily agreed to and receivd much applause.

Two Diagrammatic Drawings

The *marae* was a sacred place or shrine in Tahitian society. The pencil drawing above is believed to show Mahaiatea *marae*, which Purea and Amo built for their son's installation as *ari'i rahi* (high chief). Cook and Banks visited it on 29 June 1769. It had been partially destroyed in the recent war and the bones of many of those killed remained on the adjacent beach. Banks wrote:

Its size and workmanship almost exceeds belief ... Its form was like that of Marais in general, resembling the roof of a house, not smooth at the sides but formd into 11 steps, each of these 4 feet in hight making in all 44 feet, its leng[t]h 267 its breadth 71. Every one of these steps were formd of one course of white coral stones most neatly squard and polishd.

The drawing shows the paved square in front of the *marae* and the steps leading up to the central stone platform. The altars in the square were for offerings to Oro and in the centre is the *fare atua* or god-house, which contained an image of Oro.

The location of the second drawing (right) is less clear, although it has been suggested it also depicts Mahaiatea. It is believed that these drawings were made to show aspects of Tahitian religious practice. They are diagrams rather than accurate renderings of space, and different features can be viewed from different angles. From differences in style within the drawings, it is possible that more than one person may have contributed to them.

above
Tupaia, [Diagrammatic drawing of a *marae*], 1769
British Library, Add MS 15508, f. 16

opposite
Tupaia, [Diagrammatic drawing of a *marae*], 1769
British Library, Add MS 15508, f. 17

Tupaia, [A Scene in Tahiti], 1769
British Library, Add MS 15508, f. 14

A Tahitian Scene

This sketch is as much a representation of aspects of Tahitian life as an artwork. In the background is a longhouse, with staple food crops, including pandanus, breadfruit, banana and coconut trees and the taro plant. The attention to detail shown in drawing the different plants may indicate that it was created to illustrate to Banks key aspects of Tahitian agriculture.

In the foreground are a sailing canoe and two war canoes, with men fighting on platforms at the front. Tupaia may have drawn these to explain Tahitian warfare. Cook described the war canoes in his journal:

> Upon the fore part of all these large double Proes was placed an oblong platform about 10 or 12 feet in length, and 6 or 8 in breadth, and supported about 4 feet above the Gunels by stout carved pillars: the use of these platforms as we were told are for the Club men to stand and fight upon in time of battle, for the large Canoes from what I could learn are built mostly, if not wholly, for war, and their method of fighting is to graple one a nother and fight it out with Clubs, spears, & stones.

The diagrammatic nature of the drawing has led to suggestions that it may have been worked on collaboratively, with different elements added at different times to illustrate topics that were then being discussed.

Tupaia's Chart of the South Pacific

Banks commented as they left Ra'iatea that they 'launched out into the Ocean in search of what chance and Tupia may direct us to'. Tupaia's skills as a navigator drew on centuries of Polynesian experience of long-distance voyaging between islands, with routes preserved in oral traditions, including stories and songs. He had predicted that the *Endeavour* would find more islands directly to the south of Ra'iatea. On 14 August the ship reached Rurutu, one of the Austral group, but an attempt to land was prevented by the height of the surf and the opposition of the inhabitants, who had gathered on the beach.

Later in the voyage, Cook listed the names of Pacific islands in his journal and wrote that 'the above list was taken from a Chart of the Islands. Drawn by Tupia's own hands, he at one time gave us an Account of near 130 Islands but in his Chart he laid down only 74'. The original chart has not survived and the copy held at the British Library (overleaf) is often attributed to Cook, following a note in the lower margin. The chart attempts to document Polynesian geographical knowledge through European cartography, and scholars still debate its accuracy and meaning. The islands surrounding Tahiti are familiar, but further from the centre of the map islands become less easy to identify or match to a known location.

Several theories have been put forward to explain this. The most common theory is that the way the islands are laid out in concentric circles, with Tahiti at the centre, reflects sailing routes and distances between islands, rather than being intended as a conventional European chart. Another possibility is that mistakes in translation by Cook or lack of certainty on Tupaia's part about the location of islands further from home may have created errors in the placing of some islands. It has also been suggested that confusion over the meaning of Polynesian words for north and south led to Cook placing some islands in the wrong section.

The captions next to five of the islands are probably phonetic renderings into English characters of Tupaia's words. Johann Forster, the naturalist on Cook's second voyage, attempted to translate these in a book published in 1778 and argued that they revealed previous contact with European ships. For example, he translated the caption from Tahiti (*Meduah no te tuboona no Tupia pahei toa*) as 'Tupaya mentioned that in the lifetime of his great grandfather a hostile ship had been there' and suggested this referred to a Spanish expedition led by Pedro Fernández de Quirós in 1606. John Beaglehole, the editor of Cook's journals, made a similar translation in the 1950s ('the father of the grandfather saw a hostile ship'). Like Forster, he believed that the captions referred to visits by European ships, although he was sceptical of Forster's theory that Quirós had visited Tahiti.

More recent scholarship has questioned the assumption that the captions refer to European visits. Lars Eckstein and Anja Schwarz, in their forthcoming article, suggest that the captions refer to voyaging histories within Polynesia, including descriptions of sailing vessels, and stem from a discussion between Tupaia and a man called Topaa in New Zealand in 1770. Part of this discussion was recorded by Banks, who also added his own interpretation to the story:

Neither himself his father or his grandfather ever heard of ships as large as this [the Endeavour] being here before, but that they have a tradition of 2 large vessels, much larger than theirs, which some time or other came here and were totally destroyed by the inhabitants and all the people belonging to them killed. This Tupia says is a very old tradition, much older than his great grandfather, and relates to two large canoes which came from Olimaroa, one of the islands he has mentioned to us. Whether he is right, or whether this is a tradition of Tasmans ships… is difficult to say.

Sydney Parkinson,
[The Endeavour in stormy seas],
c. 1769
British Library, Add MS 9345, f. 16v

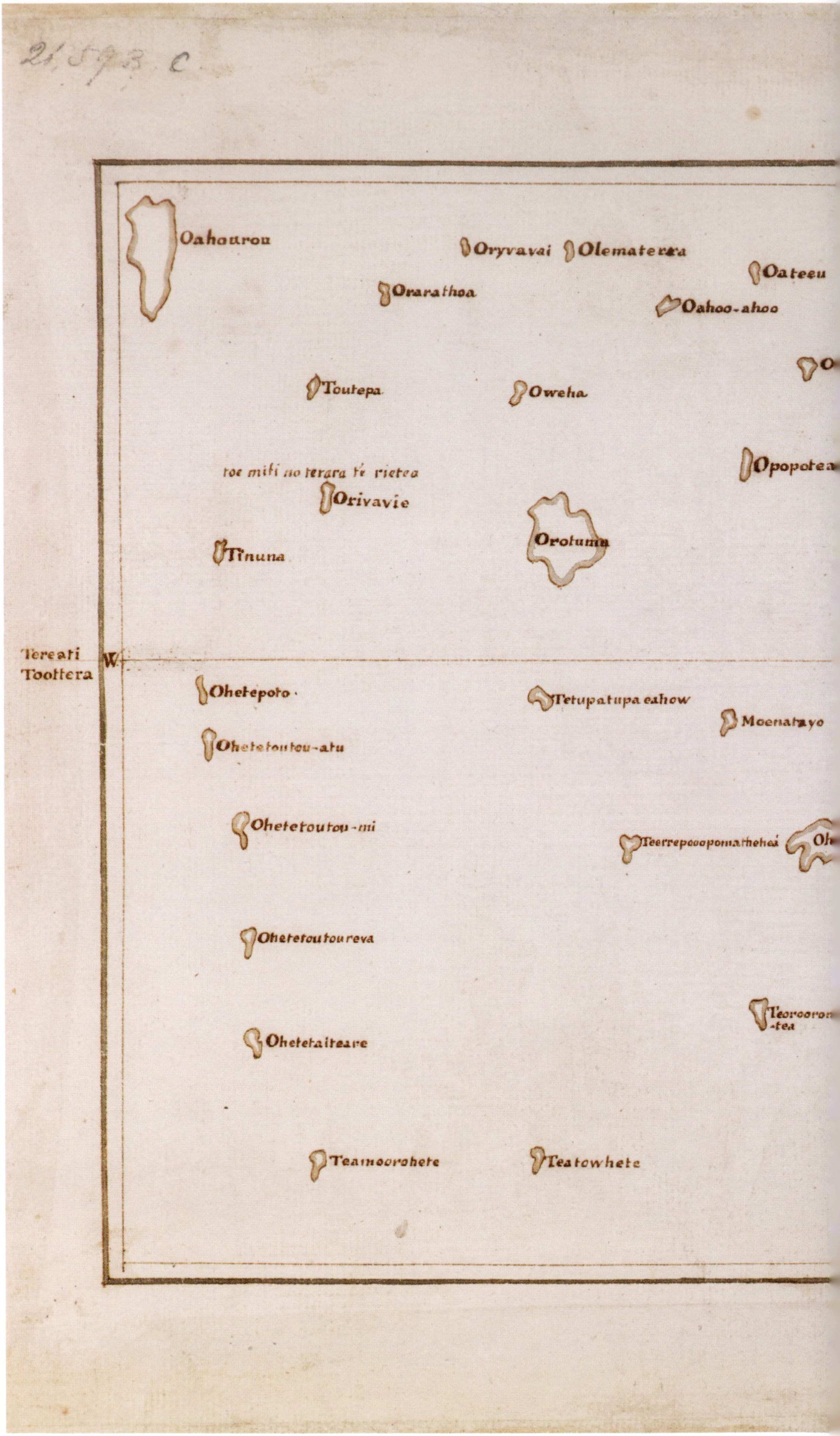

21,593. C

Oahourou

Oryvavai Olematerea

Orarathoa

Oateeu

Oahoo-ahoo

O

Toutepa

Oweha

Opopotea

toe mifi no terara te rietea

Orivavie

Orotuma

Tinuna

Tereati
Toottera

W

Ohetepoto

Tetupatupa eahow

Moenatayo

Ohetetoutou-atu

Ohetetoutou-mi

Teerrepooopomathehei

Oh

Ohetetoutoureva

Teorooron
-tea

Ohetetaiteare

Teamoorohete

Teatowhete

Attrib. James Cook, [Chart
showing the Pacific Islands,
based on information provided
by Tupaia], c. 1769–70
British Library, Add MS 21593 C

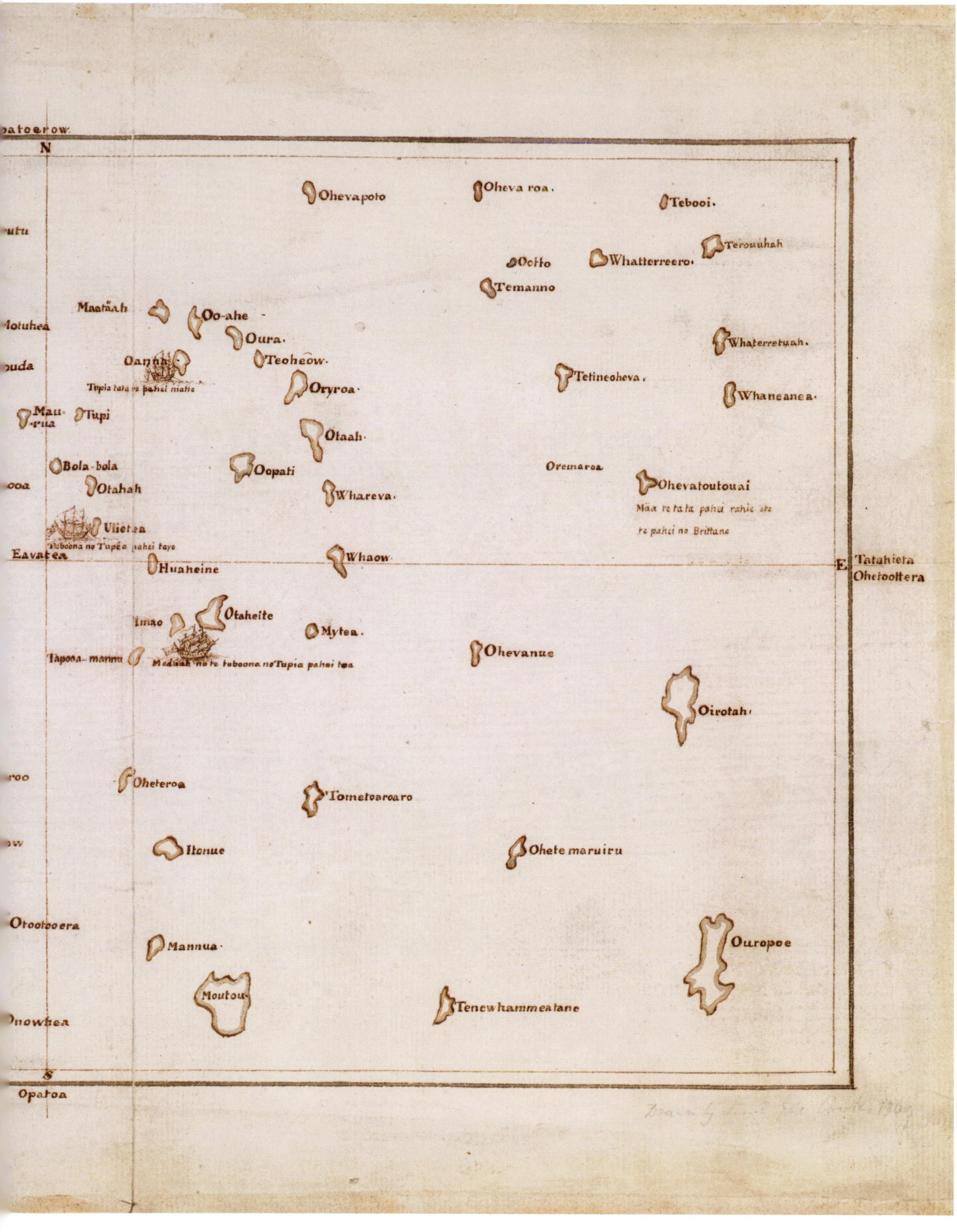

N

Ohevapoto   Oheva roa.   Tebooi.

Ootto   Whatterreero.   Terouuhah

Temanno

Maataah   Oo-ahe

Oo-ahe   Oura.   Whaterretuah.

Oannu   Teoheow.

Tupia tata te pahei matte   Tetineoheva.   Whaneanea.

Oryroa.

Mau-   Tupi
rua

Otaah.

Bola-bola   Oopati   Oremaroa

Otahah   Whareva.   Ohevatoutouai

Ulietea   Maa te tata pahei rahie ete
Tuboona no Tupia pahei tayo   te pahei no Brittane

Eavatea   Whaow.   E Tatahieta
Huaheine   Ohetoottera

Imao   Otaheite

Tapooa-mannu   Mytea.   Ohevanue

Meduah no te tuboona no Tupia pahei tea   Oirotah.

Oheteroa

Tometoaroaro

Itonue   Ohete maruiru

Otootooera

Mannua.   Ouropoe

Moutou   Tenewhammeatane

Onowhea

S

Opatoa

Aotearoa

opposite, above
Sydney Parkinson, [Three Paddles from New Zealand], 1769
British Library, Add MS 23920, f. 71a

opposite, below
Herman Spöring, 'The Head of a Canoe', New Zealand, 1769
British Library, Add MS 23920, f. 77b

Cook's orders required him to sail south from Tahiti in search of the Southern Continent, 'until you arrive in the Latitude of 40 degrees'. On 1 September a storm struck. Parkinson reported 'the sea ran mountain-high … and almost every moveable on board was thrown down, and rolled from place to place'. After reaching 40° south, Cook was to sail west in search of land until he reached the coast of New Zealand, which had been briefly visited by Abel Tasman in 1642. The distance from the Society Islands to New Zealand is approximately 2,500 miles (4,000 kilometres).

Unbeknown to Cook, the *Endeavour* was now following in the wake of voyagers who had travelled centuries before from the islands of Polynesia to the land they would name Aotearoa ('Land of the long white cloud') and which would later be known as New Zealand. While the exact dates are uncertain, archaeological evidence shows that the first people, who would later become known as Māori, had arrived by 1300 CE. Oral traditions record the journeys of a number of ocean-going *waka* (canoes), several of which arrived, as the *Endeavour* would, on the fertile east coast of the North Island.

Tupaia's arrival on the *Endeavour* and his ability to speak to the people he met in a common language was an extraordinary moment in world history, and one which some initially saw as yet another 'tall tale' from returning mariners. John Wesley, who, in January 1774, sat down by his fireside 'with huge expectation' to read the official account of Cook's voyage, was angered by 'things absolutely impossible. To instance in one, for a specimen. A native of Otaheite is said to understand the language of an island eleven hundred degrees distant from it in latitude; besides I know not how many hundreds of degrees in longitude!' Since then, the story of the original voyages has continued to astound successive generations.

Much research has taken place over recent decades into the techniques of navigation used in these journeys, supported by the re-enactment of voyages in canoes built using traditional designs. In setting out navigators used a technique known as back sighting, by which prominent landmarks behind the ship were used to ensure that its course followed the correct line, something Tupaia did to guide the *Endeavour* to islands near Tahiti. During the day, the rising and setting of the Sun gives a reference point for direction. Ocean swells, driven by trade winds, which in the Pacific remain constant for long periods of time, also provide a guide to direction. At night, knowledge of the position of the stars and planets was used to steer a course. Banks wrote in his summary of Tahiti:

In their longer Voyages they steer in the day by the Sun and in the night by the Stars. Of these they know a very large part by their Names and the clever ones among them will tell in what part of the heavens they are to be seen in any month when they are above their horizon; they know also the time of their annual appearing and disapearing to a great nicety, far greater than would be easily beleivd by an European astronomer.

The original journeys are believed to have been planned migrations. The canoes took a wide range of supplies that would be needed to establish a new homeland, including food crops that were planted on arrival. One theory is that the voyagers believed there was land to the southwest from observing the migration of birds, such as the long-tailed cuckoo and the shining cuckoo, which fly south from Polynesia in the spring and return in the autumn. The migration of whales may also have suggested this, as whales usually calve in calm waters near land. Nearer to land the formation of clouds, floating driftwood and changes to the ocean swell can indicate the presence of a coastline before it is sighted.

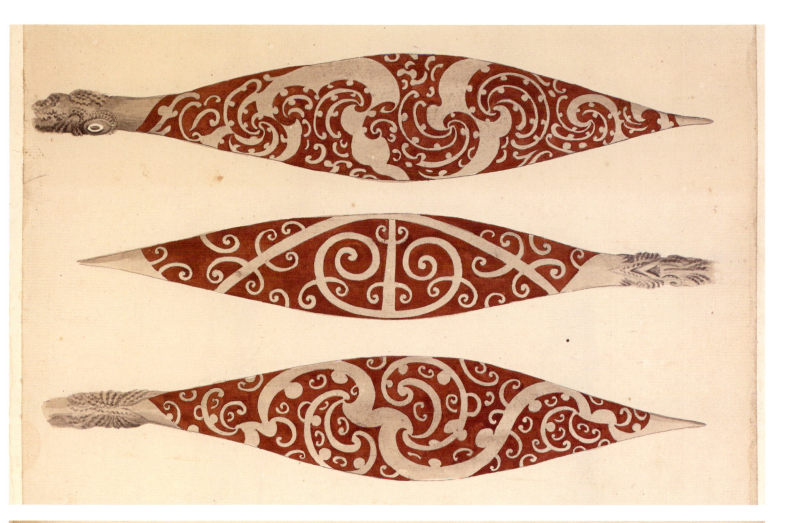

3 feet 9 inches.

2 feet

3 feet 4 inches

68½ feet in length.

5 feet 10 inches.

The Head of a Canoe.

New Zealand

James Cook, Section of a Chart
showing part of the coast of the
North Island of New Zealand,
including Tūranganui-o-Kiwa
('Poverty Bay'), 1769
British Library, Add MS 31360, f. 53

Introduction

Between Abel Tasman's departure in 1642 and Cook's arrival in 1769, a period of 127 years, there are no known visits by Europeans to New Zealand. During that time the sliver of coast mapped by Tasman, which primarily comprised the western side of the North Island, was incorporated in European maps, and sometimes shown as a northward extension of the Great Southern Continent. The Admiralty's orders stipulated that Cook was to 'explore as much of the Coast as the Condition of the Bark, the health of her Crew, and the State of your Provisions will admit'.

From late September the *Endeavour*'s company had been looking out for land, noting clumps of seaweed and floating branches as signs of the closeness of the shore. On 6 October land was sighted. The following day, as the ship sailed closer, Banks wrote up his first impressions:

> At sunset all hands at the mast head; Land still distant 7 or
> 8 leagues, appears larger than ever, in many parts 3, 4, and
> 5 ranges of hills are seen one over the other and a chain of
> Mountains over all, some of which appear enormously high.
> Much difference of opinion and many conjectures about
> Islands, rivers, inlets etc, but all hands seem to agree that
> this is certainly the Continent we are in search of.

The *Endeavour* had arrived at Tūranganui-o-Kiwa on the east coast of the North Island, which is the site of the modern city of Gisborne. On the first evening, while exploring a village on the shore that had been hastily abandoned by its inhabitants, Cook and his party heard shots and returned to the beach. The coxswain of the pinnace, which was standing offshore, had shot and killed one of four men armed with lances who had approached four boys left by Cook in a rowing boat on the shore. It is believed that the dead man was Te Maro, a chief of the Ngāti Oneone.

Over the following twenty-four hours two further incidents would take place in which the British would fire their muskets with fatal consequences. A major difficulty in reconstructing these events is the contrast between the detail in the British journal accounts and the lack of similarly detailed eyewitness accounts from the Māori perspective. The journals of Cook and Banks, which explain and justify their actions, have both been published and are consequently the most commonly cited sources for these events. The journal of one of the other British participants, William Monkhouse, is held at the British Library, and his account of the second incident, which took place the following day, is examined below.

In the third incident, Cook's decision to intercept a fishing boat in the bay, and thereby make contact in circumstances he thought he could control, led to violence when the fishermen defended themselves and the British fired muskets, killing at least two and probably four men. Three young men, the survivors of the crew of the fishing boat, were taken on board the *Endeavour*, and fed and clothed. Their names were Te Haurangi, Ikirangi and Marukauiti. Banks wrote that after one of them became upset that evening he was comforted by Tupaia. 'They then sung a song of their own, it was not without some taste, like a Psalm tune and contain many notes and semitones.'

The following morning a party went ashore. The three young men and Tupaia spoke to 150 or more men who had assembled on the opposite bank of the Tūranganui River. A man, the uncle of Marukauiti, swam across with a green bough in his hand and peace was established. The *Endeavour* sailed that afternoon from Tūranganui-o-Kiwa, which Cook called Poverty Bay due to his failure to obtain provisions there.

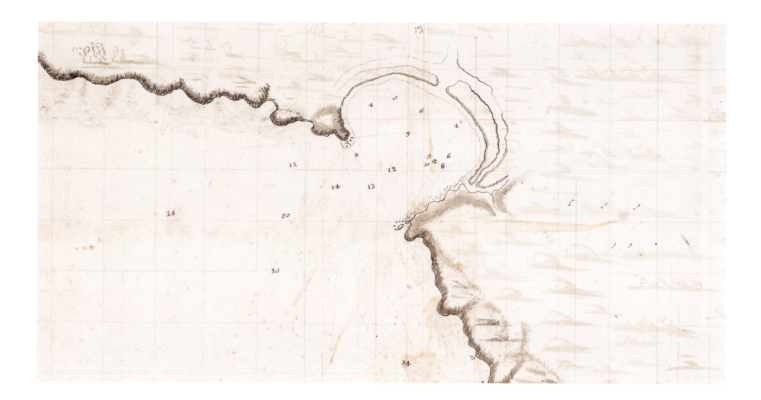

The *Endeavour* sailed south as far as 40° and then returned north. As the ship sailed along the coast, canoes put out from shore to challenge the visitors. Tupaia's role as translator and intermediary was important and he spent much time both explaining who the visitors were and asking questions about Māori society and customs. Some trade took place, with fish being exchanged for Tahitian cloth, nails and other goods, but the relationship on both sides was nervous and quickly changeable.

On 21 October, just north of Tūranganui-o-Kiwa, two old men approached the ship in canoes and were welcomed aboard with gifts. Tupaia spoke with them and they agreed that the *Endeavour* could anchor in Anaura Bay. The two men had clearly planned how to manage the visit. On the first evening Banks described how 'each family or the inhabitants of 2 or 3 houses … sat on the ground never walking towards us but inviting us to them by beckoning with one hand moved towards the breast'. Relationships soon became more relaxed, with Tahitian cloth being exchanged for food and other goods. Banks wrote that the inhabitants 'seemd pleased with observing our people as well as with the gain they got by trading with them'. Two days later, on local advice, Cook moved the ship to the neighbouring Uawa, which he called Tolaga Bay, where there was a more accessible water source. The ship stayed there for a week before continuing north.

Following encouragement from a chief called Toiawa, the *Endeavour* anchored at Te Whanganui-o-Hei in early November.

Cook and Green observed the transit of Mercury on 9 November, allowing them to establish accurately the longitude of the bay, which, somewhat inevitably, Cook called Mercury Bay. Before leaving, he also took 'formal posession of the place in the name of His Majesty'. On 19 November, opposite the mouth of a major river, two canoes came out and the visitors were invited ashore. The people in them had heard of the visit to Mercury Bay through kinship connections. Banks wrote that at a town on the river 'the people came out in flocks upon the banks inviting us in … we landed and while we stayd they were most perfectly civil, as indeed they have always been where we were known but never where we were not'.

On 29 November the *Endeavour* anchored in a bay with many islands (which Cook called 'the Bay of Islands'). A landing took place on one of the islands and, according to British accounts, the party was surrounded by two or three hundred people, many of whom were armed. The journal accounts are confused and in places contradictory. Cook wrote that after some men attempted to seize the boats he, Banks and others in the party fired small shot at them. A chief tried to rally his men and 'Dr Solander seeing this gave him a peppering with small shott'. The ship's cannons were fired over the heads of the crowd, who fled the beach. Cook, presumably with Lord Morton's instructions in mind, emphasised the limited nature of the casualties, writing that 'only one or two of them was hurt with small Shott'. An old man acted as an intermediary and peace was established, the ship staying there for several days.

Herman Spöring,
'Tolaga Bay', 1769
British Library, Add MS 23920, f. 38

Circumnavigating the North and South Islands

In December 1769 the *Endeavour* passed within a few miles of a French ship, captained by Jean de Surville, which had also been sent to explore the Pacific. Surville, whose crew were badly affected by scurvy, rounded North Cape on 17 December, during a storm that had blown the *Endeavour* out of sight of land. He landed at Tokerau, which Cook had called Doubtless Bay, and initially established good relations with the people there, trading for food and water. Relations soured when a ship's boat went missing in a storm. Surville had planned to persuade a local man to sail with him 'to obtain from him later on what information I could about this country'. When the dispute erupted he simply kidnapped a hitherto-friendly chief, who was taken aboard the ship when it sailed, and who later died on the voyage. Surville drowned in April 1770 while going ashore to seek help in Peru.

The *Endeavour*'s journey down the west coast of the North Island took only a week and no landings were made. Cook wrote that 'the great sea which the prevailing westerly winds impell upon the Shore must render this a very dangerous Coast'. The *Endeavour* explored the strait between the North and South Islands, which would later be named Cook Strait, and on 16 January 1770 anchored in a bay at the top of the South Island. Cook wrote that some people approached in canoes 'and after heaving a few stones at us and having some conversation with Tupia some of them ventured aboard'. A party went ashore and 'we found a fine stream of excellent water, and as to Wood the land here is one intire forest … we made a few hauls and caught 300 pounds weight of different sorts of fish'.

Later in the stay he described how, after gaining permission from an old man called Topaa, a post was set up at the top of a hill on Motaura Island recording the name of the ship and the dates of its visit: 'after fixing it fast in the ground hoisted therefore the Union flag and I dignified this Inlet with the name of Queen Charlottes Sound and took formal posession of it and the adjacent lands in the name and for the use of his Majesty'. It seems very unlikely that Topaa understood the nature of the ceremony or realised that Cook was claiming ownership of the land. Cook continued, 'We then drank Her Majestys hilth in a Bottle of wine and gave the empty bottle to the old man (who had attended us up the hill) with which he was highly pleased'.

The *Endeavour* left Queen Charlotte Sound in early February and initially sailed north in order to complete the circumnavigation of the North Island. From there the ship returned south, sailing down the east coast of the South Island. The people at Queen Charlotte Sound had told the British that the land to the south was an island. Nonetheless, a debate raged on board over whether the land they were passing was part of the Great Southern Continent. Banks wrote:

We were now on board of two parties, one who wishd that the land in sight might, the other that it might not be a continent: myself have always been most firm for the former, tho sorry I am to say that in the ship my party is so small that I firmly believe that there are no more heartily of it than myself and one poor midshipman, the rest begin to sigh for roast beef.

On 5 March Banks described how the land ahead turned to the west and 'was supposd by the no Continents the end of the land; towards even however it had cleard up and we Continents had the pleasure to see more land to the Southward'. On 6 March he rejoiced in the sight of land extending far to the south, writing that 'our unbelievers are almost inclind to think that Continental measures will at last prevail'. By 8 March it was clear that this

'was nothing but clouds, tho from its fixed and steady appearance nobody at that time doubted in the least its being land'.

On 9 March dawn broke to find the *Endeavour* almost wrecked on a sunken ledge of rocks. After the ship had been steered clear, Banks commented that 'the land appeared barren and seemd to end in a point to which the hills gradualy declined – much to the regret of us Continent mongers who could not help thinking this, a great swell from SW and the broken ground without it a pretty sure mark of some remarkable Cape being here'.

His journal entry on 10 March 1770 comprises one sentence: 'Blew fresh all day but carried us round the Point to the total demolition of our aerial fabric calld continent.'

The journey up the mountainous west coast of the South Island took only a week and no landings were made. Parkinson wrote of passing land 'which appeared as wild and romantic as can be conceived. Rocks and mountains, whose tops were covered with snow, rose in view one above another from the water's edge: and those near the shore were cloathed with wood, as well as some of the valleys between the hills, whose summits reached the clouds'.

On 26 March 1770 the *Endeavour* anchored at the top of the South Island. The ship had now completed a circumnavigation of both islands. In a journal entry that seems more significant now than it probably did at the time, Parkinson wrote that 'this second part of the land is about the size of the other, and the whole together is as large as Great Britain'.

RRIER ISLES

Port Charles

CAPE COLVILL

RIVER THAMES

Mercury Point

Mercury Isles

MERCURY BAY

Court of Aldermen

The Mayor

BAY OF PLENTY

White Island

Flat Island

Woody Head

Town Point

Mowtohora

CAPE RUNAWAY

Hickess Bay

EASTO

Low-land Bay

High Land point

Mount Edgcumbe

Albetross Point

Tegadoo

TOLAGA

GABLE-END FORELA

POVERTY BAY

Tettua Moire

Young Nicks Head

James Cook, [Chart of part of
the East Coast of the North
Island of New Zealand], 1769
British Library, Add MS 31360, f. 53

The Science of Cartography

Cook mapped the coast of New Zealand with help from
Charles Green, the astronomer, Robert Molyneux, the ship's
master, and other officers. The map was created on board ship,
using a technique known as a 'running survey'. The ship sailed
along the coast at a sufficient distance from shore so that
prominent coastal features could be identified. From a series of
'ship's stations', bearings would be taken to prominent coastal
features using a compass. Depth soundings were taken between
each station and sketches were made of the coastline. If the
skies were clear, latitude and longitude would be calculated
at noon each day. To ensure continuity, at least one coastal
feature visible at sunset should still be visible at dawn the
next day.

It is thought that Cook plotted each twenty-four-hour
survey from noon to noon on field sheets. Each evening he
transferred the previous day's field sheet onto a preliminary
compilation sheet (see example on page 61). Observations
made over the previous twenty-four hours were used to adjust
the positions of the ship and coast as needed. Three of these
preliminary compilation sheets survive from New Zealand.

Using data from these sheets a smaller-scale map could be
drawn showing a longer stretch of coastline. Cook used
Mercator's projection for these maps. This has a constant scale
for longitude but the scale for latitude increases further away
from the equator to allow for the curvature of the Earth's
surface.

The longitude of the coastline was established using
a method known as 'lunar distances'. Although known in
theory since the sixteenth century, this method had become
practicable with the invention of the octant in 1731 and the
sextant in 1759, instruments which allowed the measurement
of angles between the Moon and the Sun or a star. Nevil
Maskelyne, who was appointed Astronomer Royal in 1765, was
central to promoting the use of lunar distances in
navigation. In 1766 he published the first edition of his
Nautical Almanac, which included three-hourly listings of the
angular distances from the centre of the Moon to the Sun and
to nine chosen stars. Cook took Maskelyne's almanacs for 1768
and 1769 with him to the Pacific.

Abel Tasman's Journal

This drawing is from Joseph Banks's copy of Abel Tasman's journal. The original drawing, of which this is a copy, may have been by Isaac Gilsemans, who sailed with Tasman. Tasman had been sent out by the Dutch East India Company in search of new commercial opportunities. His orders stipulated that in meeting new peoples he should appear 'by no means eager for precious metals, so as to leave them ignorant of the value of the same'. The illustration shows Tasman's ships at anchor in present-day Golden Bay, on the northwest coast of the South Island. In Tasman's account, a skirmish with men in canoes led to the deaths of four of his men in a rowing boat (marked C in the picture). Following this encounter, Tasman sailed away, giving the bay the name Moordenaars Bay ('Murderer's Bay'), reflecting his view of the incident. It is not known whether any Māori were killed or injured during the encounter.

Tasman did not land in New Zealand, but he did chart the west coast of the North Island, which subsequently appeared in European maps. Tasman had initially called the coast Staten Land, after an island off Tierra del Fuego that had been believed by Jacob Le Maire to be part of the Southern Continent. Tasman chose this name because he believed he had found another part of the continent, which on European maps of that date was often shown stretching from the tip of South America to the other side of the Pacific. The Dutch later called the coastline 'Nieuw Zeeland' or 'New Seeland' after Zeeland in the Netherlands, and this name was adopted in European maps.

Page from *Copy of the journal of a voyage from Batavia, in the East Indies, for the discovery of the unknown South land, by Abel Jansen Tasman, with sketches of the coast and peoples*, 1642–3, from the collection of Joseph Banks
British Library, Add MS 8946, ff. 51v–52r

The Journal of William Monkhouse

William Monkhouse, the *Endeavour's* surgeon, wrote an account of the visit to New Zealand, which he intended to publish on his return home. The two pages overleaf, which are part of a copy believed to be from Cook's papers, describe the landing at Tūranganui-o-Kiwa (Poverty Bay) on 9 October 1769. Monkhouse's account is more detailed than those of Cook and Banks and is written in a less structured style. It gives a sense of the quickly changing nature of this first meeting, as both groups tried to make sense of what they were witnessing. Monkhouse describes how the British watched as the men on the other bank 'set up a war dance, by no means unpleasing to Spectators at a distance'. Alongside other accounts written that day, this is the first European account of the Haka: 'They seemed formed in ranks, each man jump'd with a swinging motion at the same instant of time to the right and left alternately accommodating a war song in very just time to each motion; their lances were at the same time elevated a considerable height above their heads.'

Further down the page he records that Tupaia 'no sooner called out to them than we found they understood his language – A long conversation ensued, which seemed to consist on their part of inquirys from whence we came, of complainings that we had killed one of their people, and of many expressions of doubt of our friendship'. An unarmed man swam across the river and was met by Cook who waded into the river unarmed to meet him. Monkhouse writes that 'they saluted by touching noses', the first instance of a European using the traditional Māori greeting of the *hongi*. Following this, more men began to swim across and soon the two groups were intermingling.

On the second page, Monkhouse describes how a meeting that started good-naturedly turned violent. The fact that the men brought their weapons with them evidently made the British increasingly nervous, although they also retained their own weapons. However, it seems to have been the exchange of unfamiliar European goods that caused the meeting to spin off course. Monkhouse wrote:

Active and alert to the highest degree; overjoyed with the presents they had received, but their desires by no means sated, they were incessantly upon the catch at everything they saw – every moment jumping from one foot to the other … my situation presently taught me to play the counterpart in these curious gesticulations, added to which having my bayonet fixt, I was frequently obliged to call this to my aid.

According to Monkhouse, the confrontation happened after a man teased Charles Green, the astronomer, who, turning away, had his hanger (a short sword) taken from him. The man continued to retreat with the sword 'till a musket ball dropt him'. The dead man is believed to have been Te Raakau, a chief of the Rongowhakaata tribe. Although Monkhouse does not say this, Banks recorded in his journal that it was Monkhouse who fired the fatal shot.

overleaf
Pages describing a confrontation at 'Poverty Bay' from the journal of William Monkhouse, 1769
British Library, Add MS 27889, ff. 84v–85r

9. upon the shore; however, the boats were manned and armed and a party of
gentlemen embarked for the shore — the pinnace went off the mouth of the
river in hopes of making a convenient landing within it, at which
time the natives saluted her with a loud shout — a little time was spent
in finding a place the least incommoded with surf — it was tho't proper
to have the river between us; and the moment the first party landed,
the natives now formed into a close body upon the bank of the river,
set up a war dance, by no means unpleasing to spectators at a dist-
-ance — they seemed formed in ranks, each man jump'd with a swing-
-ing motion at the same instant of time to the right and left alternately
accomodating the war song in very just time to each motion; their lances
were at the same time elevated a considerable height above their heads —

As soon as our troops were all landed we marched towards the
river having our friend Tupia a native of one of the islands we had
lately visited, with us, who no sooner called out to them than we found
they understood his language — a long conversation ensued, which seem'd
to consist of enquerys from whence we came, of complainings that we
had killed one of their people, and of many expressions of doubt of our
friendship — their pronunciation was very guttural, however Tupia
understood them and made himself understood so well that he at length
prevailed on one of them to strip of his covering and swim across —
he landed upon a rock surrounded by the tide, and now invited us to
come to him — C. Cook finding him resolved to advance no farther, gave
his musket to an attendant, and went towards him; but tho' the man saw
C. Cook give away his weapon to put himself on a footing with him, he had
not courage enough to wait his arrival, retreating into the water, how-
-ever he at last ventured forward, they saluted by touching noses, and a
few trinkets put our friend into high spirits — at this time another was
observed to strip and enter the river but he very artfully concealed his
weapon under water — he joined his countryman and was presently set
a dancing striking his thighs, and shewing the baubles he had receiv'd
to his friends on the other side. The ice was broke, and we had in a
moment six or eight more over with us all armed, except the first visiter,
with short lances — a kind of weapon we took for a paddle — and a short
hand weapon which was fastned by a string round the wrist, was about
18 inches long, had a rounded handle and thence formed into a flat elliptic
shape: this weapon, we afterwards learnt, was called pattoo.

9. before this rinforcement of troops came over, and on seing the beads di:
displayed by the two first comers we were treated with another war-
dance, so that we were now led to consider this ceremony as the effect
of opposite passions. But our new visiters kept us now in sufficient
employment — Active and alert to the highest degree; overjoyed with the
presents they had recieved, but their desires by no means sated, they
were incessantly upon the catch at every thing they saw — every moment
jumping from one foot to the other, and their eyes and hands as quick
as those of the most accomplished pickpocket: I happened to be the most
forward of our company, and was engaged with three of these young
active heroes at one time: this new manoeuvre disconcerted me for a
moment, but my situation presently taught me to play the counterpart
in these curious gesticulations, added to which, having my bayonet
fixt, I was frequently obliged to call this to my aid — on bidding them
sit down, one or other would obey for a moment — to keep them in employ=
:ment, I offered to barter for a paddle, which he was very ready to exchange
for my musket, and my refusal drew a reproach from him.
While I was thus engaged my friends behind me were not less busied;
but one of the natives having expressed a desire to have Mr. — hanger,
to avoid being too much teased Mr. — had turned about to retire, which
the man no sooner observed than he laid hold of the hanger and tore it
away, and, contented with his prize, instantly retreated towards the river.
The sufferer snapt his musket then fired a pistol — a charge of small
:shot was thrown into his back but he continued to make his escape
till a musket ball dropt him — two others instantly flew to him, I pre=
:sented my bayonet thinking they meant to carry off the hanger, but
they soon convinced me that it was a green stone pâttoo they only
wanted, which one of them tore from his wrist and retreated, while the
other endeavoured to keep me at bay — Matters were now in great con:
:fusion — the natives retiring across the river with the utmost precipi-
:tation, and some of our party unacquainted with the true state of things
begun to fire upon them by which two or three were wounded — but this
was put a stop to as soon as possible. The Natives now set up a
most lamentable noise and retired slowly along the beach.
The shot man had a human tooth hanging at one ear and a girdle of
matting about four inches broad was passed twice round his loins &
tied — He had a paddle in his hand which, tho' drawing his last breath,

Sydney Parkinson,
'Portrait of a New Zeland Man',
1769
British Library, Add MS 23920, f. 55

'Portrait of a New Zeland Man'

Soon after sailing from Tūranganui-o-Kiwa (Poverty Bay) the *Endeavour* was becalmed offshore. Several canoes approached the ship and one came alongside. Cook wrote, 'The people in this boat had heard of the treatment those had met we had had on board before and therefore came on board without hesitation'. According to Monkhouse, about twenty men came on board, while the people who remained in the canoes 'traded very freely with our People, bartering their Cloathing, weapons, and ornaments for the Otaheite Cloth'.

From descriptions in some of the journals it is believed that this portrait by Parkinson may show one of the men who went aboard the *Endeavour* that afternoon. Parkinson wrote:

Most of them had their hair tied up on the crown of their heads in a knot … their faces were tataowed, or marked either all over, or on one side, in a very curious manner, some of them in fine spiral directions like a volute [a carved spiral stonework] being indented in the skin very different from the rest.

The man wears a *hei-tiki* necklace, a long ear pendant and a flax cloak.

Although tattooing was common throughout the Pacific islands, Māori developed techniques to cut deeply into the skin, producing grooved scars and spiral motifs. The pigment used in *tā moko*, traditional Māori tattooing, was usually made from charcoal mixed with oil or liquid from plants. *Uhi* (chisels) for tattooing were traditionally made from the bones of sea birds. Comb-like instruments were also used for putting pigment into the skin. The process of *tā moko* was highly skilled, and *tohunga tā moko* (tattoo experts) were greatly respected.

A New Zealand War Canoe Bidding Defiance to the Ship

This is one of a series of drawings of canoes made by Parkinson during the visit to New Zealand. The larger canoes, which the British called war canoes, were known as *waka taua*. These could be up to about 100 feet (30 metres) long and could hold as many as a hundred people. They were beautifully carved at front and back. Warriors used them to go to battle, and the vessels were considered to be sacred. These were different to *waka tētē* (fishing canoes), which had simpler carving and were used to carry goods and people along rivers and the coast.

During the weeks the *Endeavour* spent off the east coast it was regularly challenged by canoes that put off from shore. On 13 October, four canoes approached, which were 'full of people and kept for some time under our stern threating of us all the while'. Cook, knowing that in coastal waters the *Endeavour* might need to be guided by a rowing boat ahead taking soundings, decided to try to scare away the people in the boats. He first ordered a musket shot to be fired over their heads and, when this did not have the intended effect, ordered a cannon fired wide of the boats. 'At this they began to shake their spears and Paddles at us, but notwithstanding this they thought fit to retire.'

This pattern continued during the voyage up the coast of the North Island, with canoes approaching and challenging the ship and sometimes staying to trade. Tupaia acted as intermediary, often debating and sometimes arguing with the men who approached. Banks recorded one such incident on 18 November:

Tupia who I believe guessd that they were coming to attack us immediately went upon the poop and talkd to them a good deal, telling them what if they provokd us we should do and how easily we could in a moment destroy them all. They answered him in their usual cant 'come ashore only and we will kill you all'. Well, said Tupia, but while we are at sea you have no manner of Business with us, the Sea is our property as much as yours.

Sydney Parkinson,
'New Zealand War Canoe
Bidding Defiance to the Ship',
1769
British Library, Add MS 23920, f. 50

Tupaia,
[Banks and a Maori], 1769
British Library, Add MS 15508, f. 12

Tupaia, Banks and a Māori

Tupaia's role as intermediary between Māori and British was critical in the early weeks in New Zealand. During the peacemaking at Tūranganui-o-Kiwa, Monkhouse wrote that 'Topia's name was now ecchoed incessantly'. This is Tupaia's only known drawing of New Zealand and it may have been made during or soon after the visit to Tolaga Bay, where the journal accounts refer to trade in lobsters. On 1 November, as the ship stood offshore, Banks wrote that 'at sun rise we counted 45 Canoes who were coming towards us from different parts of the shore; 7 soon came up with us and after some conversation with Tupia began to sell Muscles and lobsters of which they had great plenty'.

The drawing is believed to be the one that Banks described in his letter to Dawson Turner: 'He drew me with a nail in my hand delivering it to an Indian who sold me a Lobster but with my other hand I had a firm fist on the Lobster determined not to Quit the nail till I had Livery and Seizin of the article purchased.' (The article of trade shown is not a nail, but probably a piece of cloth.) Both participants in the exchange appear wary of each other. While Banks keeps a firm grip on his cloth the Māori has the lobster on a string, possibly to avoid it being snatched away from him. The drawing captures a sense of the drama of individual transactions where agreed rules for trade do not exist.

At Tolaga Bay, Banks wrote of Tupaia's conversation with a priest: 'they seemed to agree very well in their notions of religion only Tupia was much more learned than the other and all his discourse was heard with much attention'. Tupaia's knowledge of Hawaiki, the ancestral homeland of Māori, made his visit a unique event. Oral histories record that Tupaia preached to crowds during his stay, including using a nearby cave (now known as 'Tupaia's Cave') during rainstorms. When one of Cook's ships visited Tolaga Bay in 1773, the people there mourned the news of Tupaia's death, singing *Aue, mate aue Tupaia* – 'Departed, dead, alas! Tupaia'.

'View of the Perforated Rock at Tolaga Bay'

On the first morning at Tolaga Bay, Banks and Solander went ashore and collected 'many new plants'. Banks also described how on a walk they saw an 'extraordinary natural curiosity', which was later drawn by Parkinson:

We on a sudden saw a most noble arch or Cavern through the face of a rock leading directly to the sea, so that through it we had not only a view of the bay and hills on the other side but an opportunity of imagining a ship or any other grand object opposite to it. It was certainly the most magnificent surprize I have ever met with, so much is pure nature superior to art in these cases.

This reflected the enthusiasm for nature then current in Britain. The author Tobias Smollett wrote in 1765: 'In a fine extensive garden or park, an Englishman expects to see a number of groves and glades, intermixed with an agreeable negligence, which seems to be the effect of nature and accident … he looks for … arbours, grottos, hermitages, temples and alcoves'.

The visit was the first opportunity for Banks and his party to learn about Māori society. In contrast to his attitude at Madeira, Banks was enthusiastic over farming methods, which were highly developed on the east coast of the North Island. He wrote of the plantations: 'In them were planted sweet potatoes, cocos and some one of the cucumber kind … the first of these were planted in small lulls, some ranged in rows other in quincunx all laid by a line most regularly, the Cocos were planted in flat land and not yet appeared above ground, the Cucumbers were set in small hollows or dishes much as we do in England'. Here and elsewhere Cook and Banks planted vegetable seeds, seeking to transplant European crops to New Zealand.

The visitors described the elaborate carvings on buildings and canoes, including the curved patterns and spirals that are now synonymous with Māori art. Banks wrote that 'for the beauty of their carving in general I fain would say something more about it but find myself inferior to the task'. The visitors also collected artefacts. Banks recorded that Solander bought 'a boy's top shap'd like what boys play with in England which they made signs was to be whipped in the same manner'.

opposite
Sydney Parkinson,
'A Perforated Rock in New
Zealand' [Tolaga Bay], 1769
British Library, Add MS 23920, f. 40b

right
Charles Heaphy,
Te Horeta Taniwha, c. 1850
Alexander Turnbull Library,
Wellington, New Zealand

Te Horeta's Account

Te Horeta, also known as Te Taniwha, was a leader of the Ngāti Whanaunga, part of the Marutūahu confederation of Hauraki Gulf and Coromandel Peninsula tribes. In 1852 he described the visit of the *Endeavour* to Mercury Bay to British officials negotiating with Māori leaders over rights to mine gold in the Coromandel Peninsula. He was a child at the time of Cook's visit and an old man when his story was written down. It was later included in John White's *Ancient History of the Maori*, a multi-volume work published in the late nineteenth century:

The ship came to anchor, and the boats pulled on shore. As our old men looked at the manner in which they came on shore, the rowers pulling with their backs to the bows of the boat, the old people said, 'Yes, it is so: these people are goblins; their eyes are at the back of their heads; they pull on shore with their backs to the land to which they are going.' When these goblins came on shore we (the children and women) took notice of them, but we ran away from them into the forest, and the warriors alone stayed in the presence of those goblins; but, as the goblins stayed some time, and did not do any evil to our braves, we came back one by one, and gazed at them, and we stroked their garments with our hands …

After the ship had been lying at anchor some time, some of our warriors went on board, and saw many things there. When they came on shore, they gave our people an account of what they had seen. This made many of us desirous to go and see the home of the goblins. I went with the others; but I was a very little fellow in those days, so some of us boys went in the company of the warriors. Some

of my playmates were afraid, and stayed on shore. When we got on board the ship we were welcomed by the goblins, whom our warriors answered in our language. We sat on the deck of the ship, where we were looked at by the goblins, who with their hands stroked our mats and the hair of the heads of us children.

I and my two boy-companions did not walk about on board of the ship – we were afraid lest we should be bewitched by the goblins; and we sat still and looked at everything we saw at the home of these goblins. When the chief goblin had been away in that part of their ship which he occupied, he came up on deck again and came to where I and my two boy-companions were, and patted our heads with his hand, and he put his hand out towards me and spoke to us at the same time, holding a nail out towards us. My companions were afraid, and sat in silence; but I laughed, and he gave the nail to me. I took it into my hand and said 'Ka pai' ['very good'], and he repeated my words, and again patted our heads with his hand, and went away.

Portrait of 'Otegoowgoow'

This drawing by Sydney Parkinson is one of the most well-known and striking images from the first voyage. In Parkinson's journal the man is identified as Otegoowgoow, son of a chief from the Bay of Islands, who was wounded in the thigh with small shot during the confrontation there on 29 November 1769. Banks does not mention him by name, but describes a similar incident in which an old man brought aboard a man who had been hit in the thigh by small shot. It has been suggested that 'Otegoowgoow' may be a mishearing of the name Te Kuukuu.

The portrait shows a large comb in his hair, a greenstone ear pendant, and a *rei puta* neck ornament with eyes drawn on near the tip. Banks described the latter in his journal: 'the tooth of a whale cut slauntwise, so as something to resemble a tongue, and furnishd with two eyes; these they wore about their necks and seemd to Value almost above everything else'. The style of the facial tattoo, or *moko*, is unusual. Rather than the spiral lines being inked in, a series of vertical lines have been painstakingly tattooed across the face.

James Cook,
[Chart of New Zealand], 1770
British Library, Add MS 7085, f. 17

Cook's Chart of New Zealand

This is James Cook's completed chart of New Zealand. It shows the course of the *Endeavour* as it circumnavigated the North Island and then the South Island. The number of names on the east coast of the North Island compared to those on the rest of the chart reflects the time the *Endeavour* spent on that coast and the number of landings made. In the title Cook uses the Dutch name ('New Zeland') and also attempts to record the Māori names for both islands. The name he gives to the South Island ('Tovypoenammu') is a reasonably close rendering of Te Wai Pounamu, meaning 'the waters of greenstone'. The name given to the North Island ('Aeheinomouwe') is less obviously derived from the Māori name, Te Ika a Maui (meaning 'the fish of Maui'), although it is possible this is an attempt to spell it phonetically.

  The chart contains two notable mistakes, both caused by poor visibility as the *Endeavour* sailed past. Firstly, 'Banks Island' on the east coast of the South Island is actually a peninsula. Secondly, 'Cape South' at the bottom of the South Island is shown as a peninsula but is actually part of an island, now called Stewart Island.

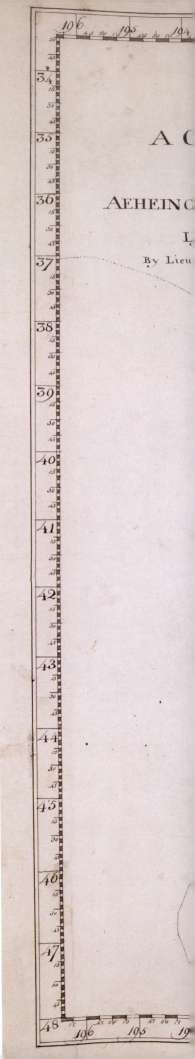

OF NEWZELAND

ISLANDS OF

E and TOVYPOENAMMU

he SOUTH SEA.

mmander of the ENDEAVOUR BARK 1770

Var. 11.25 E.

Three Kings

Cape Maria Van Diemen

CAPE NORTH

Var. 12.4 E

Sandy Bay

Knuckle P.t

Doubtless Bay

Cavelles Isles

Mount Camel

Mount Pococke

Cherry Isl.t

Cape Brett

Bay of Islands

Poor Knights

Bream Rd.

Bream Bay

Hen & Chickens

Bream Head

Hauraki Isl.

P.t Rodney

Cape Charles

False Bay

Mercury Isles

Mercury Point

Mercury Bay Var. 11.9 E

Court of Aldermen

The Mayor

White Isl.t

Runaway

Woody Head

BAY OF PLENTY

Flat Island

Gannet Isle.

Low Land B.

Hicks's Bay

Island P.t

Albertross Point

Mount Edgecumbe

Tegadoo

Tolago

Springs Isl.t

Gable-end Foreland

Poverty Bay

Young Nicks Head

Portico-metto

Sugarloaf Isles

Sugarloaf Point

Table Cape Var. 14.36 E

Var. 14.15 E

Isle of Portland

Mount Egmont

C. Kidnappers

Cape Egmont

Black Head

COOK's

C. Turnagain

Cape Farewell

ALPS

Rocks Point

East P.t

Stephens

Stephens Isl.

Blind Bay

Admiralty Bay

Cloudy bay

Queen Charlottes Sound

Blackson

C. PALLISSER

Cape Campbel

STRAIGHTS

Var. 15.4 E

Cape Foul-wind

Snowey Mountains

Lookers on

Var. 15.30 E

Gores Bay

Banks's Island

Var. 14.39 E

ALPS

istaken Bay

btfull Harb.

Point

CAPE

C. Saunders

S.W. Bay

S.E. Bay

Bench Island

Var. 15.16 E

Traps

Var. 16.29 E

Var. 16.36 E

Var. 16.34 E

Australia

This entry in the *Endeavour*'s log records the arrival of the ship at 'Stingray Harbour', which Cook later called Botany Bay, in April 1770. Cook later wrote up a more detailed account in his journal.
British Library, Add MS 27885, f. 21

Introduction

One of the most enduring myths about James Cook is that he 'discovered Australia'. In fact, he was not the first person, the first European or even the first Briton to arrive there. The first people are believed to have arrived in Australia from South East Asia about 60,000 years ago. A skeleton of an adult male discovered at Lake Mungo in New South Wales is believed to date from 42,000 years ago. A fragment of a charcoal rock painting found at Nawarla Gabarnmang in the Northern Territory has been carbon-dated as being 28,000 years old. Estimates of the population of Australia in the eighteenth century vary, but a figure of 750,000 has been suggested by recent research. There are believed to have been several hundred tribal or kinship groups and about 250 different languages.

The first European ship known to have visited Australia was the *Duyfken*, captained by Willem Janszoon, which was sent by the Dutch East India Company to explore the coast of New Guinea and reached the northern tip of the Australian mainland in 1606. Over the following century the Dutch would explore and map much of the north, west and south coasts of the land they called 'New Holland'. The first English ship to visit Australia was the *Cygnet*, which arrived on the northwest coast in 1688. William Dampier, one of those on board, published *A New Voyage Round the World* in 1697, the first book in English to describe Australia in detail. He returned in 1699, and, in 1703, published *A Voyage to New Holland*, which included plates depicting Australian plants, birds and fish.

On 31 March 1770 Cook called his officers together to discuss the options for returning home from New Zealand. He wrote in his journal:

To return by the way of Cape Horn was what I most wish'd because by this route we should have been able to prove the existence or non-existence of a Southern Continent ... But the condition of the ship in every respect was not thought sufficient for such an undertaking. For the same reason the thoughts of proceeding directly to the Cape of Good Hope was laid a side especially as no discovery of any moment could be hoped for in that rout. It was therefore resolved to return by way of the East Indies by the following rout: upon leaving this coast to steer to the westward until we fall in with the East Coast of New Holland and than to follow the deriction of that Coast ... untill we arrive at its northern extremity.

On 19 April 1770 the *Endeavour* arrived near the southern tip of the east coast of Australia. The following day Banks wrote: 'The country this morn rose in gentle sloping hills which had the appearance of the highest fertility, every hill seemed to be cloth'd with trees of no mean size; at noon a smoak was seen a little way inland and in the Evening several more'. Cook sailed north looking for a harbour where supplies could be taken on board. On 28 April he wrote that the ship had arrived at a bay 'which appeard to be tollerably well shelterd from all winds into which I resolved [sic] to go'.

The *Endeavour* anchored in the bay and a party set out in the boats towards a group of people and huts on the shore. The area around the landing site formed part of the lands of the Gweagal people. Two Gweagal men, armed with spears and stones, opposed the landing and, according to the British accounts, a standoff lasting a quarter of an hour ended with small shot being fired at the legs of the men, injuring one of them. The men retreated after throwing spears at the British. The landing party found the camp deserted, apart from a group of children hiding in one of the huts. They left some beads in the hut with the children and took away the spears they found in the camp, in

Weekd:	Mo:	Winds	Remarks &c in Nº
Aprl 1770			

gentle breazes and settled weather. at 3 pm
anchor'd in 7 fathom water in a bay which I calld
Sting-Ray Harbour the south point bore SE
and the north point East distant from the south shore
1 Mile we saw several of the natives on both
sides of the Harbour as we came in and a few hutts domen
and children on the north shore opposite to the place
where we anchor'd and where I soon after landed with
a party of men accompaned by Mr Banks Dr Solander
and Tupia — as we approach'd the shore the natives
all made off except two men who at first seem'd
resolved to oppose our landing. we endeavourd to
gain their consent to land by throwing them some
nails beads &c ashore but this had not the disired
effect for as we put in to the shore one of them threw
a large stone at us and as soon as we landed they
threw 2 darts at us but the foreing of two or three
musquets load with small shott they took to the
woods and we saw them no more we found here a few
poor hutts made of the bark of trees in one of which
were hid 4 or 5 Children with whom we left some
strings of Beads &ca after searching for fresh
water without success except a little in a small
hole dug in the sand — we embarqued and went
over to the north point of the Bay where in
coming in we saw several of the natives but
when we now landed we saw no body but we here
found some fresh water which came trinkling
down and stood in Pools among the rocks but
as this was troublesome to get at I sent a party of
men ashore in the morning abreast of the ships
to dig holes in the sand by which means we
found fresh water sufficient to water the ships
after breakfast I sent some empty casks ashore to
fill and a party of men to cut wood and went
my self in the Pinnace to sound and explore the
Bay in the doing of which I saw several of the
natives who all fled at my approach —

Sunday 29

This engraving, which was published in the official account of the voyage, shows the ship beached at Endeavour River following its collision with the Great Barrier Reef.

Engraving by William Byrne after Sydney Parkinson
British Library, Add MS 23920, f. 36

order to disarm the inhabitants. The *Endeavour* stayed a week in the bay, during which time little direct contact was made with the local people, who observed the British from a distance. Cook displayed the Union flag ashore every day and called the harbour 'Botany Bay' owing to the number of plants Banks and Solander collected.

The *Endeavour* sailed on 6 May 1770. A few miles further up the coast Cook described another bay 'wherein there apperd to be safe anchorage which I call'd Port Jackson'. The ship sailed on, not stopping to investigate the bay that in 1788 would become the site of the British penal colony that later grew into the modern city of Sydney.

Further north the waters became increasingly difficult to navigate. Initially this was due to offshore islands and shallow water, meaning that boats had to be sent ahead to sound the depth. However, the *Endeavour* was gradually moving into a natural funnel created by the Australian coast to the west and the Great Barrier Reef to the east. By the time the danger was realised, the ship was already many miles north with no easy route to open sea.

On 11 June the *Endeavour* ran into the reef. In Cook's words, 'the Ship Struck and stuck fast'. For several hours it looked as though it would sink. However, after jettisoning ballast and equipment, including several cannons, it was successfully re-floated. A sail was dropped down the outside of the hull, a practice known as fothering, which staunched the leak by using external water pressure to hold it in place. The ship was slowly steered towards shore, and boats were sent ahead to look for a harbour. In a river estuary further north the *Endeavour* was hauled ashore and the breach in the hull examined. Banks commented that 'here providence had most visibly worked in our favour, for it was in great measure pluggd up by a stone which was as big as a mans fist'.

For the first few weeks at 'Endeavour River' no contact was made with the inhabitants, although fires were observed in the distance. It is likely that the Guugu Yimithirr people, who lived in the area, also observed the visitors from a distance. In early July a group of Guugu Yimithirr men visited the camp and friendly relations were established over the following days. Parkinson described the men as 'very merry and facetious' while

Banks wrote that they 'seemed to have lost all fear of us and became quite familiar'. Good relations ended abruptly in a dispute over some turtles which had been killed by the British and were laid on the *Endeavour*'s deck, leading to the firing of shots by the British after their campsite was set on fire. A reconciliation took place soon after, brokered by an old man, but this was the last time the two groups met.

The *Endeavour* sailed on 11 August 1770. The following day a party landed on an island and Cook climbed to the top of a hill. He wrote that 'to my mortification I discovered a Reef of Rocks laying about 2 or 3 Leagues without the Island, extending in a line NW and SE farther than I could see'. He also saw several breaks in the reef, through which the ship might be taken into the open sea. To stay close to the shore meant a continual risk of grounding in shallow water and the possibility of the reef joining with the land further north and boxing the ship in. After consulting with his officers he decided to attempt to cross the line of the reef through a passage of open water.

A boat was sent ahead to sound the depths and on 14 August the ship crossed into open sea. Cook, however, wished to remain in sight of shore as he hoped to prove that there was a channel between the east coast of Australia and New Guinea. This tempted him to sail too close to the reef on 16 August and, with a strong wind from the east, the ship began to be drawn onto it. Banks described the reef as:

> a thing scarcely known in Europe or indeed any where but in these seas … It is a wall of Coral rock rising almost perpendicularly out of the unfathomable ocean, always overflown at high water commonly 7 or 8 feet, and generaly bare at low water; the large waves of the vast ocean meeting with so sudden a resistance make here a most terrible surf breaking mountain high.

Over the following twenty-four hours the crew fought a desperate battle with the tides. Banks wrote that 'a speedy death was all we had to hope for'. As the ship was drawn closer Cook decided to risk sailing through an opening in the reef. On 17 August this was achieved, prompting him to muse on the vicissitudes of an explorer's reputation:

> The world will hardly admit of an excuse for a man leaving a Coast unexplored he has once discover'd, if dangers are his excuse he is than charged with Timorousness and want of Perseverance and at once pronounced the unfitest man in the world to be employ'd as a discoverer; if on the other hand he boldly incounters all the dangers and obstacles he meets and is unfortunate enough not to succeed he is than charged with Temerity and want of conduct.

In late August the northern tip of Australia was reached. Cook landed on a small island, called Bedanug by the local people, which he called 'Possession Island'. Here, in the name of George III, he 'took possession of the whole Eastern Coast from the above Latitude down to this place by the name of New South Wales'. He wrote it 'gave me no small satisfaction' to be able 'to prove that New-Holland and New-Guinea are 2 Separate Lands or Islands'.

'Two of the Natives of New Holland Advancing to Combat'

This is an engraving from the published version of Sydney Parkinson's journal, which appeared after his death. It is the best-known image of Cook's landing at Botany Bay and is believed to be based on a lost original drawing by Parkinson, although the engraver may well have added elements of his own interpretation. Banks described how, as the *Endeavour*'s boats approached the shore, two men came down on to the rocks 'shaking their lances and menacing, in all appearance resolvd to dispute our landing to the utmost tho they were but two and we 30 or 40 at least'. The picture is regularly used to illustrate the famous standoff between the two men and Cook's landing party.

Earlier, as the ship entered the bay, Banks observed a group of men standing on rocks at the entrance, 'threatening and menacing with their pikes and swords – two in particular who were painted with white, their faces seemingly only dusted over with it, their bodies painted with broad strokes drawn over their breasts and backs resembling much a soldiers cross belts, and their legs and thighs also with such like broad strokes drawn round them'. It seems possible that the original Parkinson drawing, if indeed it existed, was based on this episode rather than the more famous confrontation on the beach. It is also possible that it was a composite of both.

Plate XXVII

Parkinson del.

T. Chambers Sc.

Two of the Natives of New Holland, Advancing to Combat.

Tupaia,
[Australian Aborigines
in Bark Canoes], 1770
British Library, Add MS 15508, f. 10

Fishing from Canoes

This drawing by Tupaia shows two canoes, in one of which a man is using a three-pronged spear to catch a fish. Banks described how, as the *Endeavour* entered the bay, he observed 'four small canoes' under the southern headland:

In each of these was one man who held in his hand a long pole with which he struck fish, venturing with his little imbarkation almost into the surf. These people seem'd to be totaly engag'd in what they were about: the ship passd within a quarter of a mile of them and yet they scarce lifted their eyes from their employment; I was almost inclind to think that attentive to their business and deafned by the noise of the surf they neither saw nor heard her go past.

Fishing canoes were also observed later in the stay. Banks described them in his journal:

A peice of Bark tied together in Pleats at the ends and kept extended in the middle by small bows of wood was the whole embarkation, which carried one or two, nay we once saw three people, who movd it along in shallow water by setting with long poles; and in deeper by padling with padles about 18 inches long, one of which they held in each hand. In the middle of these Canoes was generaly a small fire upon a heap of sea weed, for what purpose intended we did not learn except perhaps to give the fisherman an opportunity of Eating fish in perfection by broiling it the moment it is taken.

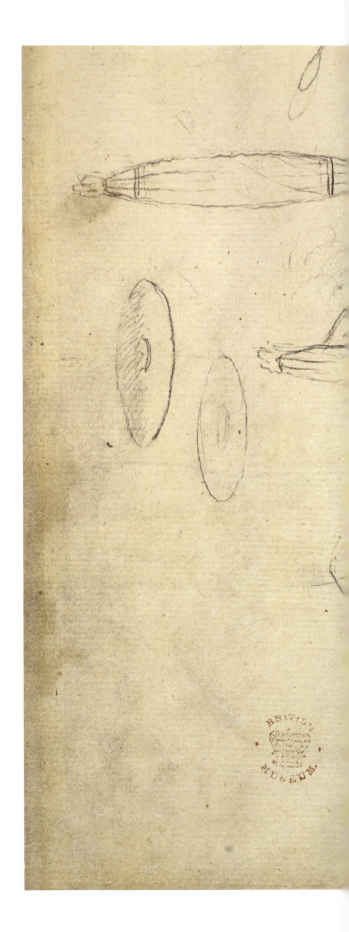

Sydney Parkinson's Sketchbook

These pencil drawings are from Sydney Parkinson's sketchbook
and are believed to have been made during the week the
Endeavour stayed at Botany Bay. The page shows ten sketches in
total, including men, canoes, shields and a hut. The sketches
would have been intended to prompt Parkinson's memory when
working later on finished artworks. One of the sketches shows a
man with a spear and spear thrower; the latter, which was
commonly used on the east coast, projected the spear with
greater force than if thrown by hand.

Parkinson's sketches capture the fleeting nature of encounters
between the British and the people of the bay after the initial
confrontation. On the evening of the second day, fifteen men
approached the watering party. According to Banks, 'they sent
two before the rest, our people did the same; they however did
not wait for a meeting but gently retired'. A number of similar
encounters took place over the following days. On 1 May ten
men, armed with spears and swords, visited the watering place.
Cook wrote: 'I follow'd them alone and unarm'd some distance
along the shore but they would not stop untill they got farther
off than I choose to trust my-self'.

James Cook, 'Botany Bay in New
South Wales', *c.* 1770
British Library, Add MS 31360, f. 32

Cook's Chart of Botany Bay

This chart is believed to have been drawn by Cook using an
earlier sketch, which is also held at the British Library. The exact
date of the finished copy is unclear, although the inclusion of
the name New South Wales means that it must have been
completed after the ship left Australia. The chart notes fresh
water in several locations, includes soundings of the main
channels, and gives British names to locations.

Banks had been collecting specimens throughout his time on
shore and on 3 May he commented that 'our collection of Plants
was now grown so immensely large that it was necessary that some
extraordinary care should be taken of them'. He spread a sail in
the sunlight on the shore and spent the day drying the plant
specimens. Parkinson recorded that 'from the number of curious
plants we met with on shore, we called the bay Botany Bay'.

The names on the chart illustrate the change that this short
visit would bring about. The two headlands are still called Cape
Banks and Cape Solander. The landing site is now part of
Kamay Botany Bay National Park, the dual name acknowledging
a history of human settlement in the area dating back many
thousands of years before the arrival of the *Endeavour*.

Charles Praval,
[Drawing thought to show a man
of the Guugu Yimithirr people],
1770–71
British Library, Add MS 15508, f. 15

Endeavour River

The place Cook called Endeavour River was part of the lands of the Guugu Yimithirr people. The first meeting between the British and the Guugu Yimithirr took place on 10 July 1770, when two men approached in a canoe. Banks wrote that after encouragement 'by degrees they ventured almost insensibly nearer and nearer till they were quite along side, often holding up their lances as if to shew us that if we used them ill they had weapons and would return our attack'. As in the Society Islands and New Zealand, Tupaia took the role of intermediary, although here, like the Europeans, he could not speak the language.

Tupia went towards them; they stood all in a row in the attitude of throwing their Lances; he made signs that they should lay them down and come forward without them; this they immediately did and sat down with him upon the ground. We then came up to them and made them presents of Beads, Cloth &c which they took and soon became very easy, only Jealous if any one attempted to go between them and their arms. At dinner time we made signs to them to come with us and eat but they refusd; we left them and they going into their Canoe paddled back to where they came from.

Over the following days the two groups got to know each other. On 11 July Banks wrote that he was introduced to some new men, one of whom was called Yaparico, noting, 'Tho we did not yesterday observe it they all had the Septum or inner part of the nose bord through with a very large hole in which one of them had stuck the bone of a bird as thick as a mans finger and 5 or 6 inches long'. The following day more men visited: 'they introduc'd their strangers (which they always made a point of doing) by name'. This drawing by Charles Praval, who joined the ship at Batavia later that year, is believed to be based on a lost drawing

by Parkinson and may show one of the men who visited the camp in July 1770.

Following the dispute in mid-July the local men stopped visiting the camp. However, towards the end of the stay Banks wrote that a sailor who had strayed from the main party met two men and a boy in the woods:

At first he was much afraid and offered them his knife, the only thing he had which he thought might be acceptable to them; they took it and after handing it from one to another returned it to him. They kept him about half an hour behaving most civilly to him, only satisfying their curiosity in examining his body, which done they made signs that he might go away which he did very well pleased.

opposite

Sydney Parkinson,
Kangaroo
Natural History Museum, London

below

Sydney Parkinson,
Ipomoea Indica, unfinished
watercolour
Natural History Museum, London

The Kangaroo

This is one of two sketches by Parkinson, which are the first European drawings of the kangaroo. Soon after the landing at Endeavour River a party exploring inland saw an animal 'as large as a greyhound, of a mouse colour and very swift'. The following day Banks saw the same animal and wrote: 'What to liken him to I could not tell, nothing certainly that I have seen at all resembles him … instead of going upon all fours this animal went only upon two legs, making vast bounds'. A few days later he recorded that 'our second lieutenant who was shooting today had the good fortune to kill the animal that has so long been the subject of our speculations':

> *To compare it to any European animal would be impossible as it has not the least resemblance of any one I have seen. Its fore legs are extremely short and of no use to it in walking, its hind again as disproportionaly long; with these it hops 7 or 8 feet at each hop in the same manner as the Gerbua, to which animal indeed it bears much resemblance except in size, this being in weight 38 lb and the Gerbua no larger than a common rat.*

The following day the kangaroo was cooked and eaten, Cook reporting that he 'thought it excellent food' and Parkinson that it tasted like the flesh of a hare 'but has a more agreeable flavour'.

A popular myth is that the word *kangaroo* comes from an Australian Aboriginal word meaning 'I don't know'. In fact, the word is believed to be based on the Guugu Yimithirr word *gangurru*, which refers to a species of kangaroo.

Ipomoea Indica

This drawing by Sydney Parkinson depicts *Ipomoea Indica* or blue morning glory, a specimen of which was collected in the Endeavour River area. In order to work quickly and to conserve paint, Parkinson often just included examples of colour in his botanical drawings. This allowed finished artworks to be created later in Britain by copying the colours in the original drawings.

James Cook,
'A Chart of part of the Sea Coast
of New South Wales', 1770
British Library, Add MS 7085 f. 39

A Chart of the *Endeavour*'s Course

This chart shows the northern part of the east coast of Australia. It illustrates the convoluted and sometimes tortured journey of the *Endeavour* on the last stage of its journey up the east coast, as it passed first outside then back inside the Great Barrier Reef. The site of the collision that almost ended the voyage is marked, as is the landing site at Endeavour River. The dotted line on the coast north of Endeavour River indicates that after sailing outside the reef the ship was too far offshore for the coastline to be charted. 'Providential Channel' marks the point at which the *Endeavour* avoided a second collision by sailing through a gap in the Great Barrier Reef. It was on one of the 'Possession Isles' that Cook claimed the east coast of Australia.

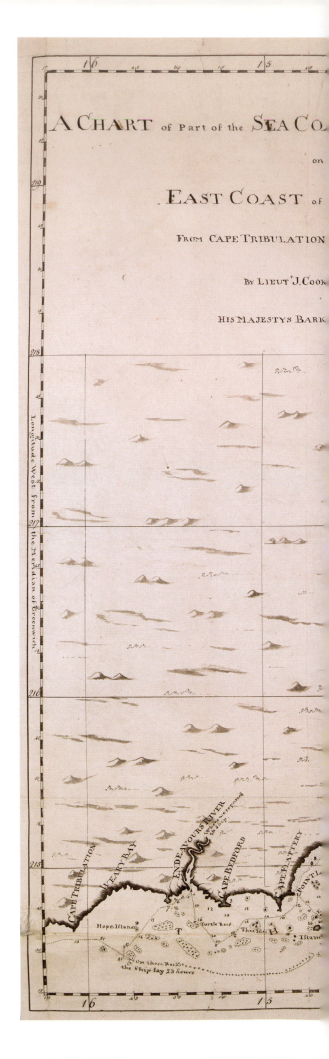

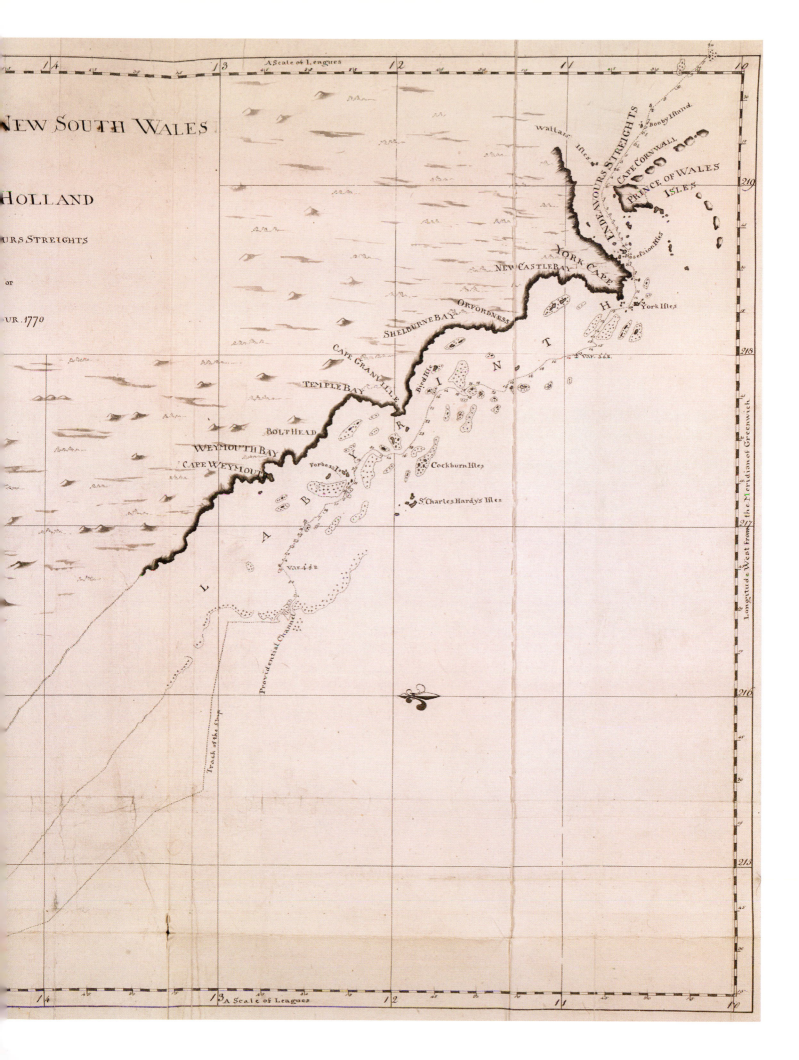

NEW SOUTH WALES

HOLLAND

URS STREIGHTS

or

UR. 1770

Wallais Isles

INDEAVOURS STREIGHTS

Booby Island

CAPE CORNWALL

PRINCE OF WALES ISLES

YORK CAPE

Hosselton Isles

NEW CASTLE BAY

York Isles

ORFORDNESS

Var. Isles

SHELBURNE BAY

CAPE GRANVILLE

Bird Isle

TEMPLE BAY

BOLT HEAD

WEYMOUTH BAY

CAPE WEYMOUTH

Forbess Isle

Cockburn Isles

St. Charles Hardy's Isles

Var. 4½ E.

Providential Channel

Track of the Ship

Longitude West from the Meridian of Greenwich

Possession Island

Cook's decision to claim the east coast of Australia for the British Crown is probably the most controversial action of his career. Historians still debate the reasons why he did this, in apparent contradiction of the Admiralty's instructions to claim 'convenient situations in the country' with the consent of the inhabitants. In the passage describing the claiming ceremony, he wrote that he was confident that the coast 'was never seen or viseted by any European before us', which had been one of the Admiralty's criteria for claiming land. In journal entries written at around the same time he also seems to echo broader philosophical debates in Britain and Europe, probably reflecting discussions on board ship with Banks and others.

In his book *Two Treatises of Government* (1690), the English philosopher John Locke had argued that God had given the Earth to man to make use of: 'it cannot be supposed he meant it should always remain common and uncultivated. He gave it to the use of the industrious and rational (and labour was to be his title to it)'. In a famous and controversial section, he argued, 'as much land as a man tills, plants, improves, cultivates, and can use the product of, so much is his property'. Locke argued that the inhabitants of North America, which was then being colonised by the British, lacked political or economic organisation (at least to European eyes) and therefore lived in a 'state of nature'. Locke's views provided a philosophical underpinning to colonisation in North America and later in other parts of the world.

Soon after claiming the east coast of Australia Cook wrote a summary of the land and its people in his journal. In this, whether consciously or not, he seemed to echo Locke's views:

We are to Consider that we see this Country in the pure state of Nature. The Industry of Man has had nothing to do with any part of it and yet we find all such things as nature hath

bestow'd upon it in a flourishing state. In this Extensive Country it can never be doubted but what most sorts of Grain, Fruits, Roots & c of every kind would flourish here were they once brought hither, planted and cultivated by the hand of Industry; and here are Provender for more Cattle at all seasons of the year than ever can be brought into this Country.

Locke's views were famously attacked by Jean-Jacques Rousseau who, in his 1755 work *A Discourse upon Inequality*, also posited the existence of a 'state of nature'. Rousseau argued:

The first Man, who, after enclosing a Piece of Ground, took it into his Head to say, This is Mine, and found People simple enough to believe him, was the true Founder of Civil Society. How many Crimes, how many Wars, how many Murders, how many Misfortunes and Horrors, would that Man have saved the Human Species, who pulling up the Stakes or filling up the Ditches should have cried to his Fellows: Be sure not to listen to this Imposter; you are lost, if you forget that the Fruits of the Earth belong equally to us all, and the Earth itself to nobody!

In his summary of Australia Cook also echoed Rousseau's views. He wrote that the inhabitants 'may appear to some to be the most wretched people upon Earth, but in reality they are far more happier than we Europeans':

Being wholy unacquainted not only with the superfluous but the necessary Conveniencies so much sought after in Europe, they are happy in not knowing the use of them. They live in a Tranquillity which is not disturb'd by the Inequality of Condition: The Earth and sea of their own accord furnishes

*them with all things necessary for life, they covet not
Magnificent Houses, Household-stuff &c, they live in a
warm and fine Climate and enjoy a very wholesome Air, so
that they have very little need of Clothing … in short they
seem'd to set no Value upon any thing we gave them, nor
would they ever part with any thing of their own for any
one article we could offer them; this in my opinion argues
that they think themselves provided with all the necessarys of
Life and that they have no superfluities.*

In his journal there is no evidence that Cook saw a contradiction
in his espousal of these two views, both of which were conventions
of European thought during his time. Neither view was
informed by detailed knowledge of the culture and societies of
the people of the east coast of Australia. As Cook himself wrote
at Botany Bay, 'we could know but very little of their customs as
we never were able to form any connections with them'.

Samuel Calvert, after John
Alexander Gilfillan, 'Cook taking
possession of the Australian
Continent on behalf of the British
Crown AD 1770, under the name
of New South Wales' from
The Illustrated Sydney News,
December 1865. The picture
reflects widespread Victorian
colonial attitudes. While Cook
speaks, a group of Aboriginal
people perform menial tasks in
the foreground. The man serving
drinks to Cook's right may be the
artist's depiction of Tupaia.

left
John Wells, after Drummond,
'A View of Batavia', *c.* 1800,
aquatint
British Library, P494

opposite
R. B. Godfrey, after Sydney
Parkinson, 'The Lad Taiyota,
Native of Otaheite, in the Dress
of his Country'. Engraving
published in Parkinson, *A journal
of a voyage to the South Seas*,
1773, plate IX, facing page 66
British Library, L.R.294.c.7

Batavia

From Australia, the *Endeavour* sailed north to Batavia, the centre of the Dutch empire in the East Indies, where arrangements were made for it to be repaired in the dockyards. Tupaia had fallen ill with scurvy but, Banks wrote, on arrival at Batavia his 'spirits which had long been very low were instantly raisd by the sights which he saw, and his boy Tayeto [Taiato] who had always been perfectly well was almost ready to run mad':

Houses, Carriages, streets, in short every thing were to him sights which he had often heard describd but never well understood, so he lookd upon them all with more than wonder, almost made with the numberless novelties which diverted his attention from one to the other he danc'd about the streets examining every thing to the best of his abilities. One of Tupia's first observations was the various dresses which he saw worn by different people; on his being told that in this place every different nation wore their own countrey dress He desird to have his, on which South Sea cloth was sent for on board and he cloathd himself according to his taste.

The Dutch had modelled Batavia on the towns of Holland, even down to the canals which crisscrossed its centre and acted as natural reservoirs of disease. On 28 October Banks commented that 'the Seamen now fell sick fast so that the tents ashore were always full of sick'. On 5 November William Monkhouse died. On 9 November Taiato died and on 11 November he was followed by Tupaia. In all seven men died at Batavia.

On the journey across the Indian Ocean fever again took hold. On 24 January 1771 John Truslove, one of the marines, died. The following day Herman Spöring died. On 27 January Sydney Parkinson and John Ravenhill, a sailmaker, both died. On 29 January Charles Green died. Two men died on 30 January and four on 31 January. Over the following weeks Cook continued to record deaths in his journal. On 27 February he listed the deaths of three seamen, Henry Jeffs, Emanuel Pharah and Peter Morgan, but noted that the rest of the crew 'are in a fair way of recovering'.

The *Endeavour* passed Land's End in Cornwall on 10 July 1771 and anchored off the Kent coast on 13 July. Cook had written to the Admiralty from Batavia that 'the discoveries made in this Voyage are not great' and explaining he had 'failed to discover the so much talk'd of southern continent (which perhaps do not exist)'. In a personal letter to John Walker, written soon after his return, he echoed this, writing: 'I however have made no very great Discoveries'.

Plate IX

S. Parkinson del.

R. B. Godfrey Sculp.

The Lad Taiyota, Native of Otaheite, in the Dress of his Country.

BETWEEN THE VOYAGES (1771–72)

Honours and Controversy

Soon after the return of the *Endeavour*, John Hawkesworth was appointed by the Admiralty to write the official account of the voyage, which would also cover the earlier British expeditions to the Pacific of John Byron and Samuel Wallis. Hawkesworth was provided with copies of the records of all three expeditions, including the journals of both Cook and Banks. Public interest in the story was such that he was able to sell the copyright in the book for £6,000. James Boswell and Samuel Johnson discussed the book's potential importance:

> **JOHNSON.** '*Sir, if you talk of it as a subject of commerce, it will be gainful; if as a book that is to increase human knowledge, I believe there will be not much of that. Hawkesworth can tell only what the voyagers have told him; and they have found very little, only one new animal, I think.*'
>
> **BOSWELL.** '*But many insects, Sir.*'
>
> **JOHNSON.** '*Why, Sir, as to insects, Ray reckons of British insects twenty thousand species. They might have staid at home and discovered enough in that way.*'

The book became a bestseller on publication in June 1773 and proved the cause of much controversy, which is believed to have contributed to Hawkesworth's premature death later that year. In the introduction he dismissed the idea that providential intervention by God had saved the *Endeavour* from being wrecked on the Great Barrier Reef, leading to accusations of blasphemy. In using the journal accounts he was fulsome in his descriptions of the sexual freedoms of the Pacific islands, leading to allegations of immorality and sensationalism. He was also creative in his editorial approach, 'improving' passages where he thought necessary to illustrate a moral and placing the words of one person in the mouth of another.

The main rival to the official account was the journal of Sydney Parkinson, published by his brother Stansfield. In a long preface he attacked Banks, alleging that he had withheld Sydney's journals, drawings and other personal effects from his family. Parkinson's manuscript journal is not known to survive. According to Banks, he had lent Stansfield 'some loose sheets of a journal, which seemed to be only foul copies of a fair journal that I never found', on condition these were returned. Stansfield placed an advert in the press offering a hundred guineas for information on the missing journal and drawings, stating that 'there is great reason to believe that they have been secreted by some person or persons for his or their own emolument'. In this way he claimed to have 'procured, by purchase, loan and gift, not indeed the fair copy of my brother's journal, but so many of his manuscripts and drawings, as to enable me to present the following work, in its present form, to the public'. Not long after Sydney's journal was published Stansfield was committed to an insane asylum, where he died soon after.

If the dispute with Stansfield Parkinson damaged Banks's reputation for honesty, then Hawkesworth's book did much to promote the view of him as a sexual adventurer. After its publication a number of anonymous articles and poems appeared in the press concerning his time in Tahiti, often linking him amorously with Purea. These included a poem entitled 'An

R. B. Godfrey, after Sydney
Parkinson, 'The Head of a Native
of Otaheite [sic] with the Face
curiously tataow'd'. Engraving
published in Parkinson, *A journal
of a voyage to the South Seas*,
1773, plate VII, facing page 24
British Library, L.R.294.c.7

An imagined depiction of the
1767 meeting between Purea
('Oberea') and Samuel Wallis
from Hawkesworth, *An account
of the voyages undertaken by the
order of His Present Majesty for
making discoveries in the
Southern Hemisphere*, 1773
British Library, G.7449

Hawkesworth's attempts to draw moral lessons also led to
ridicule. The author of the above poem wrote that 'the people of
Otaheite are remarkable for their *fine feelings*, which generally
produce a copious effusion of tears upon every affecting
occasion'. Cook did not see Hawkesworth's account until his
return from the second voyage. Boswell records meeting him at
a dinner in April 1776, when he 'set me right as to many of the
exaggerated accounts given by Dr Hawkesworth'.

Although he did not achieve the same prominence as Banks,
Cook also became a public figure following the return of the
Endeavour. He was presented to George III and began to be
invited to fashionable social occasions. The musician and author
Charles Burney wrote in his memoirs: 'I had the honour of
receiving the illustrious Captain Cooke to dine with me in
Queen-square, previously to his second voyage round the world'.
Cook and Burney discussed Bougainville's published account of
his voyage to the Pacific, and Burney wrote that this:

> *Made me desirous to know, in examining the chart of M. de
> Bougainville, the several tracks of the two navigators; and
> exactly where they had crossed or approached each other.
> Captain Cooke instantly took a pencil from his pocket-book,*

Epistle from Oberea, Queen of Otaheite, to Joseph Banks',
which drew on a real incident, recounted by Hawkesworth, in
which Banks's clothes had been stolen from Purea's tent:

> *Oft on thy lips, those lips of love, I hung,*
> *To hear thee greet me in my native tongue;*
> *Meetee atira [kiss me], sweetly you exprest,*
> *Your eyes all-eloquent explain'd the rest.*
> *Say fondest youth, canst thou forget the night,*
> *When starting from your sleep in wild affright;*
> *Rise Oberea, rise my Queen, you said,*
> *Some thief has stol'n my breeches from my head.*

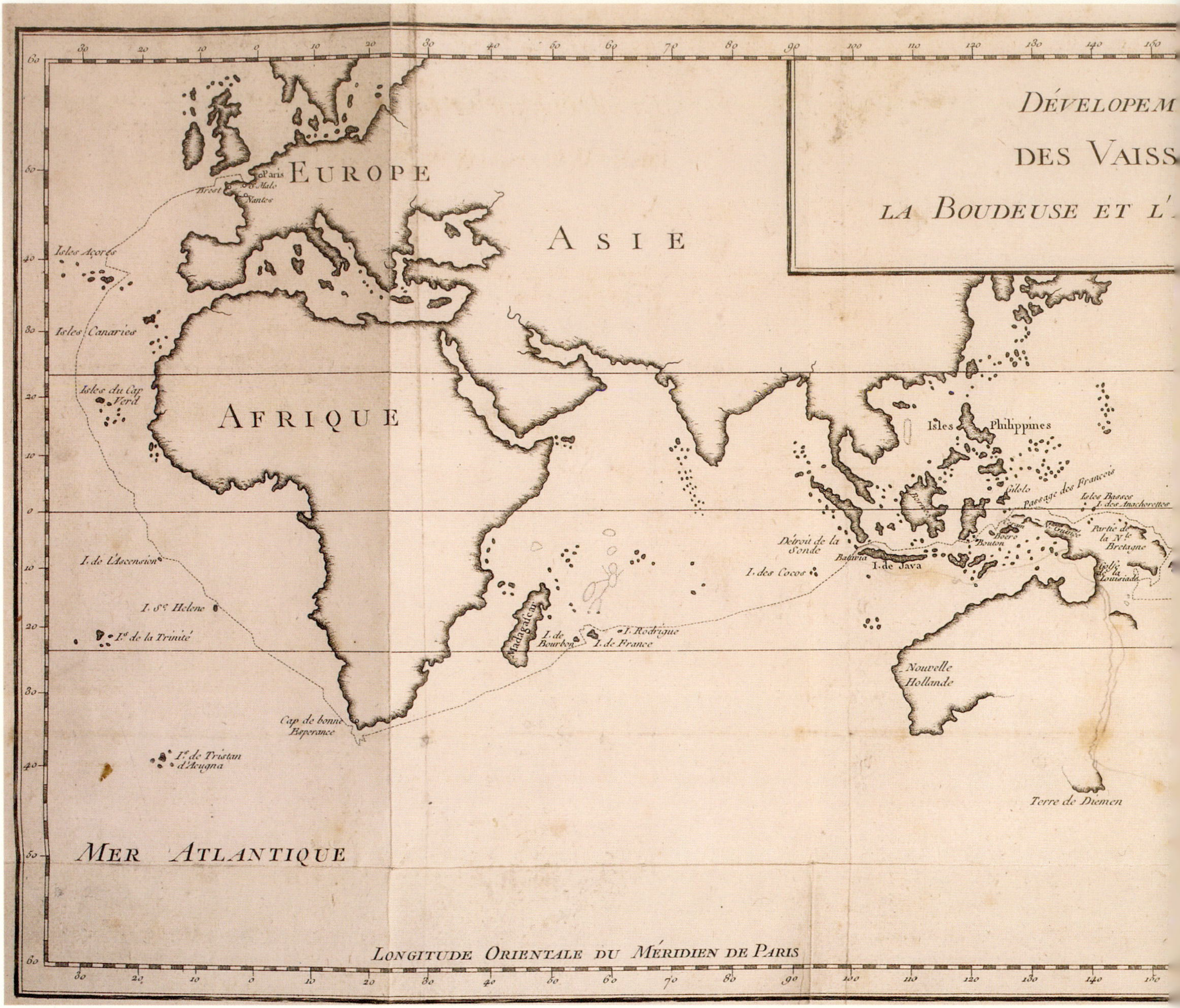
Dévelopem
des Vaiss
la Boudeuse et l'
Europe
Asie
Afrique
Isles Açores
Isles Canaries
Isles du Cap Verd
Paris
Brest
S. Malo
Nantes
Isles Philippines
Passage des François
Gilolo
Isles Basses
I. des Anachorettes
Partie de la N^{le} Bretagne
Golfe de la Louisiade
Boero
Bouton
Détroit de la Sonde
Batavia
I. de Java
I. des Cocos
I. de L'Ascension
I. Ste Helene
I^{le} de la Trinité
Madagascar
I. de Bourbon
I. Rodrigue
I. de France
Nouvelle Hollande
Cap de bonne Esperance
I^{le} de Tristan d'Acugna
Terre de Diemen
Mer Atlantique
Longitude Orientale du Méridien de Paris

and said he would trace the route; which he did in so clear and scientific a manner, that I would not take fifty pounds for the book. The pencil marks having been fixed by skim-milk, will always be visible.

Burney's copy of the map is now held in the British Library. As he predicted, the route sketched by Cook that evening can still be seen. Although, in charting New Zealand and the east coast of Australia, Cook had filled in the largest areas of previously unmapped coast in the South Pacific, an even larger area of the ocean remained unknown in Europe and speculation continued that the Great Southern Continent awaited discovery there. In a postscript to his journal, written on his return to Britain, Cook had proposed a second voyage to search this area and either prove or disprove the existence of the continent. In autumn 1771 he was commissioned by the Admiralty to lead this expedition. Banks also planned to join the voyage.

Banks arrived at Deptford in spring 1772 with an entourage comprising around fifteen people, including Daniel Solander, the painter Johann Zoffany, the scientist Dr James Lind and two French horn players. The Navy Board initially refused, then submitted to, a request to alter the superstructure of Cook's ship, the *Resolution,* to create additional cabins. Cook noted ruefully the instruction to 'build a round house or couch for my accommodations so that the Great Cabbin might be

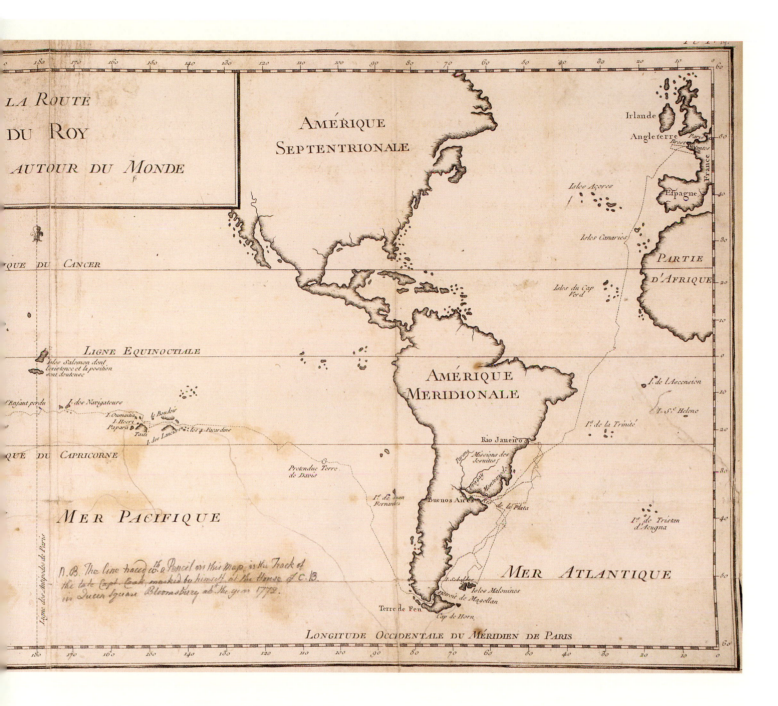

La Route
du Roy
Autour du Monde

Amérique
Septentrionale

Tropique du Cancer

Ligne Equinoctiale

Isles Salomon dont
l'existence et la position
sont douteuse

L'Enfant perdu   I. des Navigateurs

I. Oumaitia
I. Hoert
Papara   I. Boudoir
Tati   I. des Lanciers   les 4 Facardins

Tropique du Capricorne

Mer Pacifique

Amérique
Meridionale

Rio Janeiro

Paraguay   Missions des
Jesuites

Uruguay
Montevideo

Buenos Aires   Rio de la Plata

I. de Juan
Fernandez

N.B. The line traced w.th a Pencil on this map, is the Track of
the late Capt. Cook marked by himself, at the House of C.B.
in Queen Square Bloomsbury in the year 1772.

Ligne des Antipodes de Paris

I. St. Aldrice
Détroit de Magellan   Isles Malouines

Terre de Feu
Cap de Horn

Mer Atlantique

Longitude Occidentale du Méridien de Paris

Irlande
Angleterre
Espagne   France

Isles Açores

Isles Canaries

Partie
d'Afrique

Isles du Cap
Verd

I. de l'Ascension

I. Ste Helene

I. de la Trinité

I. de Tristan
d'Acugna

appropriated to the use of Mr Banks alone'. When the ship was launched it listed badly, Charles Clerke describing it as 'the most unsafe ship I ever saw or heard of'. The Admiralty ordered the alterations reversed, leading to a public row with Banks and his supporters.

Following the intervention of the Prime Minister, Lord North, and George III, the Admiralty prevailed. Accepting defeat, Banks chartered a ship to take his party (minus Zoffany) to Iceland instead, as the nearest place where 'the whole face of the country [was] new to the Botanist & Zoologist'. On the way he spent several weeks exploring the Hebrides, motivated by the belief that an ancient Scottish culture and way of life, rapidly disappearing elsewhere, was preserved there. This was to become

a well-trodden path. Thomas Pennant had visited in 1769 and in 1773 Boswell and Johnson would make their famous tour, Johnson describing the Highlands as 'a country on which perhaps no wheel has rolled'. The drawings from the expedition show the work of artists who, but for the dispute with the Admiralty, would have accompanied Cook to the Pacific.

Cook's pencil sketch of the
Endeavour's route on the first
map in Bougainville's *Voyage
autour du monde*, 1771
(Charles Burney's copy)
British Library, C.28.I.10

[Fingal's cave on the
island of Staffa]
British Library, Add MS 15510, f. 42

Interest in the Scottish Highlands had been increased by the
publication of James Macpherson's *Fingal, an Ancient Epic Poem,
in Six Books* in 1762, supposedly English translations of Gaelic
works by the legendary warrior-bard Ossian. The poems were
written in Homeric style and seemed to show the existence of
a sophisticated literary culture in ancient Scotland. Macpherson
claimed to have collected the poems from surviving manuscripts
and oral traditions but was soon assailed with accusations of
having fabricated them. The controversy over the Ossian poems
became a motif for the problem of disentangling authentically
surviving knowledge from modern mythology, especially where
written records do not survive. In his account of his 1773 visit to
the Highlands, Samuel Johnson wrote that 'tradition is but
a meteor, which, if once it falls, cannot be rekindled', and
cautioned 'if we know little of the ancient highlanders, let us
not fill the vacuity with Ossian'.

In contrast, Banks was a believer in the authenticity of the
poems, enthusing over visiting 'the Land of Heroes once the seat

of the Exploits of Fingal and the mother of the romantick
Scenery of Ossian'. The highlight of the visit was a trip to
Staffa, where there was a cave containing 'pillars like those
of the Giant's Causeway'. The artists made drawings of its
basalt columns while the scientists investigated and described
its structure. In an echo of his comments on the arch at Tolaga
Bay, Banks wrote:

*Compared to this what are the cathedrals or the palaces
built by men? … Where is now the boast of the architect!
Regularity, the only thing in which he fancied himself to
exceed his mistress, Nature, is here found in her possession,
and here it has been for ages undescribed. Is not this the
school where art was originally studied, and what has been
added to this by the whole Grecian school.*

According to Banks, he was told by the local guide that the cave
was named after Fingal. He wrote: 'How fortunate that in this

John Cleveley Jr.,
[The geyser at Haukadalur]
British Library, Add MS 15511, f. 37

John Cleveley Jr.,
'Icelandic woman in
her bridal dress'
British Library, Add MS 15512, f. 17

cave we should meet with the remembrance of that chief, who's existence, as well as that of the whole *Epic* poem is almost doubted in *England*'.

The expedition continued to Iceland, then a Danish colony, arriving at the end of August. The scientists observed and recorded Iceland's unique geology and natural phenomena, while the artists drew scenes of Icelandic life. Banks, perhaps seeking to emulate Macpherson, collected books and manuscripts containing Icelandic history and mythology, which were later lodged in the British Museum. In September the party climbed Mount Hekla, the famous volcano, known since its eruption in 1104 as the 'gateway to hell'. On the summit they found steam emerging and the ground too hot to sit on. During the visit they also observed the eruptions of the Great Geyser at Haukadalur, and Lind measured the height of its water spouts using a quadrant. A ptarmigan shot by Banks was cooked in the boiling waters in seven minutes. At Thjorsardalur they bathed in the hot springs.

The party returned to Britain in autumn 1772. Banks's decision not to return to the Pacific with Cook meant that he was able to build his relationships to a range of powerful individuals and organisations in London. In 1773 he was appointed by George III as his botanical advisor, in which role he would oversee the development of Kew Gardens as a centre for the transplantation of crops across the British Empire. In 1774 he was invited to join the Council of the Royal Society, which paved the way for his election as President only four years later. In 1774 he was also elected to the Society of Dilettanti, a club for wealthy scholars and collectors. By the time the *Resolution* returned to Britain in 1775, Banks had become a figure at the heart of the British establishment.

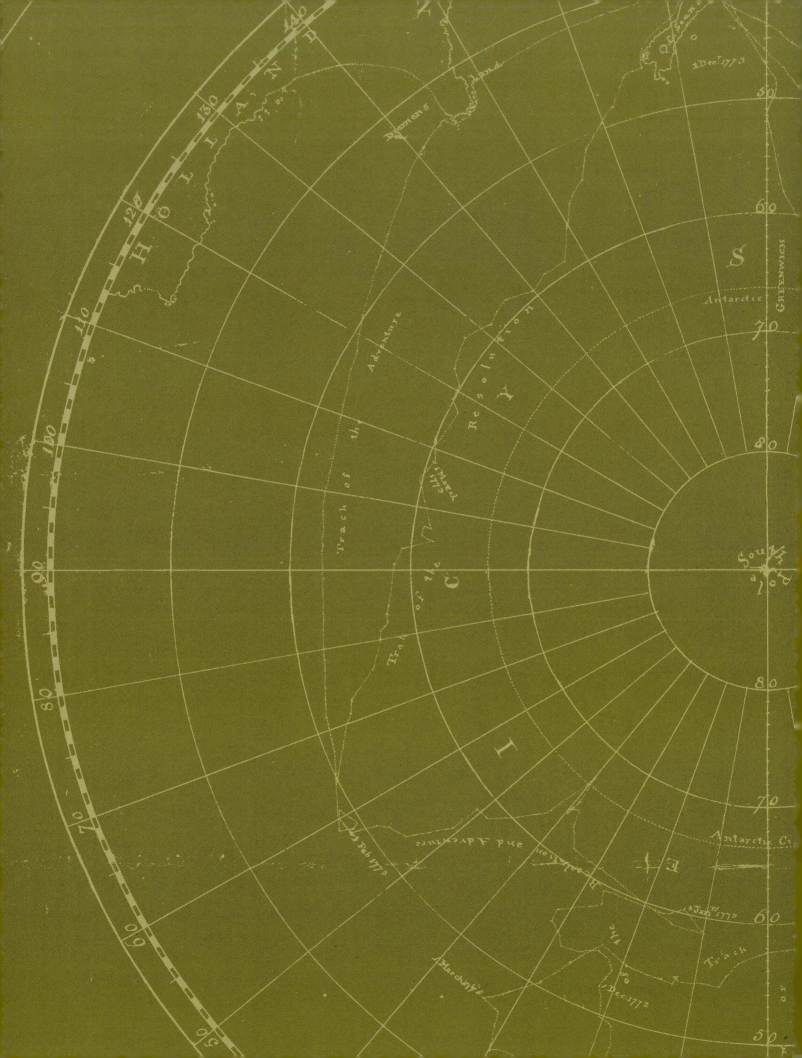

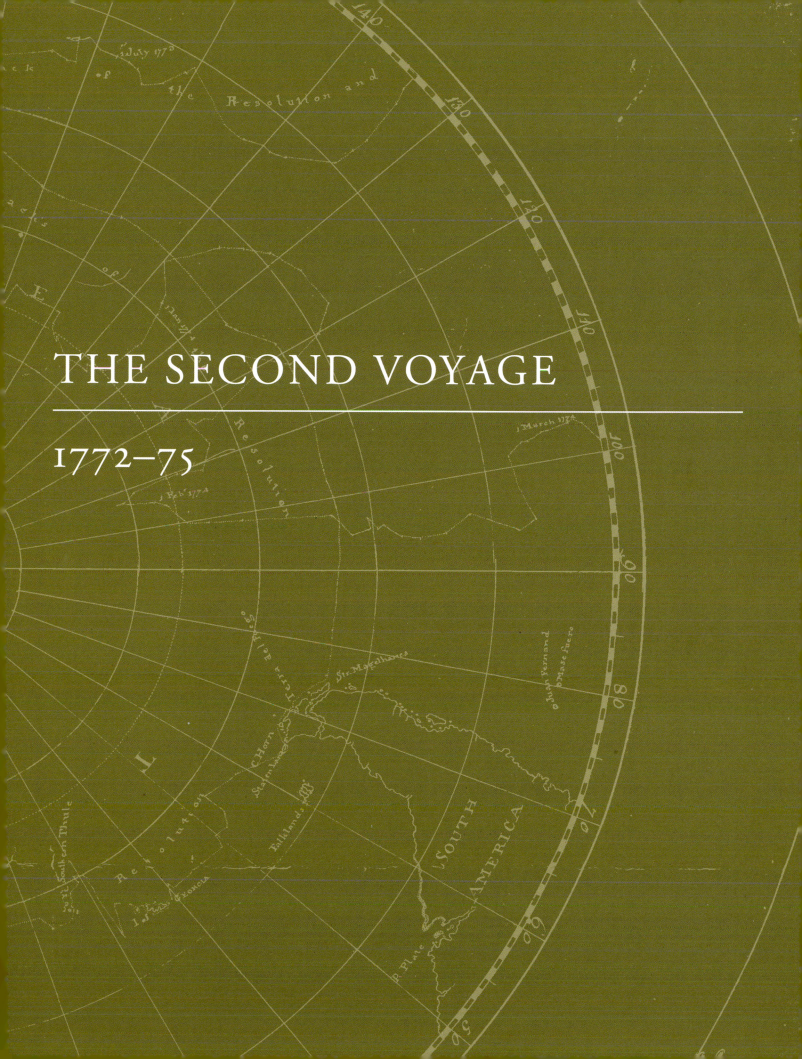

THE SECOND VOYAGE

1772–75

The Instructions

The Admiralty's instructions for the second voyage stipulated that Cook was to search for 'that Southern Continent which has so much engaged the attention of Geographers & former Navigators'. He was to sail south from the Cape of Good Hope in search of land sighted by a French expedition in 1738 and believed by some to be the tip of the continent. After this he was to use his own judgement and search for land:

Either to the Eastward or Westward as your situation may then render most eligible, keeping in as high a Latitude as you can, & prosecuting your discoveries as near to the South Pole as possible; And you are to employ yourself in this manner so long as the condition of the Sloops, the health of their Crews, & the State of their Provisions will admit of it …

Cook commanded the *Resolution* while Tobias Furneaux, who had sailed with Wallis to Tahiti, commanded the *Adventure*. Like the *Endeavour*, both ships were former Whitby colliers. In searching for the Southern Continent, and ultimately proving its non-existence, Cook would make two long journeys into the Antarctic and, during the winter months, two long circuits of the South Pacific, charting the location of many islands previously visited by Europeans but until then not accurately plotted on the map. The scientists on board were the first to observe and describe the Antarctic seas.

The expedition took with it copies by Larcum Kendall and John Arnold of John Harrison's chronometer. This was a scientific instrument designed to keep time accurately at sea, making it possible to calculate longitude east or west from Greenwich much more easily than by the method of lunar distances used on the first voyage. Harrison had created a series of prototypes since the 1730s and the current version, H-4, had proved successful in trials in the Atlantic. The chronometer made it easier to chart the location of land accurately, a major step forward in mapping the Pacific and thereby opening it up to European ships.

left
This map, which is from George III's collections, shows how the Great Southern Continent was imagined in Europe. The small areas of coastline highlighted in colour depict the only known sightings of land in this area.
British Library, Maps K.top.4.60

above
Copies of Harrison's chronometer made by John Arnold
The Royal Society, London

The Scientific Party

Johann Forster, who was appointed by the Admiralty as naturalist, was born near Danzig in 1729 and ordained as a Lutheran pastor in 1751. During the Seven Years' War his home town was occupied by Russian troops and in 1765 he was commissioned by the Tsar's government to survey the Volga region. In 1766 he moved to Britain where he worked as a lecturer and writer, quickly becoming a patriotic British subject. For Forster, Britain had 'a mild Government, where every thing is upon an equitable footing, where laws prevail & no despotic power takes place, there the meanest of the Subjects is allways treated with tenderness & care, vice is punished, & virtue is rewarded, & courage perseverance, & good conduct meet always with encouragement'.

Forster had departed from Plymouth with a message from Linnaeus ringing in his ears: 'It is to you that all who love and treasure natural science should look'. He was the most well-read of the scientists who travelled on the voyages and was self-consciously a follower of Francis Bacon, declaring that experiment was 'the firmest & only basis possible for getting at truth'. He was also quite sensitive to perceived insults. William Wales, the *Resolution*'s astronomer, later wrote 'before

we reached New Zealand the first time, there was scarce a man in the ship whom he had not quarrelled with on one pretence or other'. Forster's son Georg accompanied him on the voyage as an assistant and natural history artist. The Swedish naturalist Anders Sparrman, a pupil of Linnaeus, was recruited as a second assistant when the ship called at Cape Town.

William Wales was, like Cook, a Yorkshireman born in humble circumstances. He was a skilled mathematician and was employed in 1766 by Nevil Maskelyne, the Astronomer Royal, to help prepare the first edition of his *Nautical Almanac*. In 1768 he was sent to Hudson's Bay to observe the transit of Venus for the Royal Society. His wife Mary was the youngest sister of Charles Green, the astronomer who had helped Cook chart New Zealand. Wales was appointed by the Board of Longitude to sail on the *Resolution*, along with William Bayly, who sailed as astronomer on the *Adventure*. Wales was responsible for the copy of H-4 made by Larcum Kendall, which was designed as an exact replica of the original. He and Bayly were also responsible three cheaper copies made by John Arnold, although these were soon found to be less reliable.

William Hodges

William Hodges was appointed by the Admiralty as the official artist. He was born in London in 1744 and was the son of a blacksmith. In 1755 he was enrolled in William Shipley's school, where he learned to draw. An idea of the ethos of the school is given by the aims of the Society for the Encouragement of Arts, Manufactures and Commerce, which Shipley founded in 1754: 'To embolden enterprise, to enlarge science, to refine Art, to improve Manufactures, and extend our Commerce; in a word, to render Great Britain the school of instruction, as it is already the centre of traffic to the greatest part of the world.'

After leaving school Hodges worked as an apprentice for Richard Wilson, the landscape painter, before becoming an independent artist. Unlike the artists on the *Endeavour*, Hodges survived the voyage to the Pacific and was later employed by the Admiralty to supervise the engravings for the official account and to produce a series of oil paintings. Many of these works depict Pacific societies and landscapes in classical form, drawing heavily on Greek myths of the Golden Age. Hodges's use of light and colour is striking, whether in the subtle shadings of the pen and ink drawings he made on the voyage or in the bright contrasts of the oil paintings he completed in London.

In 1779 Hodges went to India, where he was commissioned by the British governor Warren Hastings to make drawings of landscapes and buildings. Unlike in his Pacific drawings, Hodges portrayed India as an ancient civilisation now in decline, often showing ruined buildings as relics of a former greatness and contrasting these with the supposedly corrosive effects of luxury.

On his return to London Hodges published a book of engravings of his Indian work. He established his own studio in Mayfair and was elected to the Royal Academy.

In 1794 Hodges put on a self-financed exhibition, which featured two huge paintings entitled *The Effects of Peace* and *The Consequences of War*. This took place at the height of the French Revolutionary Wars and, following criticism from the Duke of York that the paintings showed 'sentiments not suited to the public tranquillity', it was closed down. Hodges retreated to Brixham in Devon, where he abandoned painting and opened a bank, which soon failed. He died in 1797.

William Daniell, after George Dance, *William Hodges RA*, 1808, etching
National Portrait Gallery, Canberra

The First Crossing of the Antarctic Circle

The ships left Plymouth on 13 July 1772, calling at Madeira and the Cape Verde Islands before arriving at the Cape of Good Hope on 30 October. There they took on supplies and the chronometers were tested. As the ships sailed south from the Cape the temperature dropped and the weather worsened. Of conditions on the *Adventure* Furneaux wrote: 'The sea making a continual breach over us, and the decks leaky not only wet peoples cloaths, but the beds on which they lay, so that they were extremely fatigued, cold and helpless'. On 30 November Forster described the impact of a storm:

> The people had not yet been prepared for such weather, &
> therefore did the rolling of the Ship much damage, chairs,
> glasses, dishes, plates, cups, Saucers, bottles etc were broken:
> the Sea came in one or the other cabin & made all the
> inside wet, or a lose box or cask stove out some bulkhead &
> brought down a cabin. In short the whole Ship was a
> general scene of confusion & desolation.

Throughout the voyage Forster quoted passages from the *Aeneid* in Latin in his journal to dramatise scenes he encountered. On 30 November his chosen passage was: 'Then came the cries of the men and the groaning of the rigging. Darkness, like night, settled on the sea, and all the elements threatened the crew with death at any moment'.

On 10 December the first floating ice was seen in the sea. The next day Forster described 'a large mass of Ice quite cubical or like a parallellepipedon, of a huge size' and calculated, based on knowledge of icebergs in the North Atlantic, that it was '1600 feet deep, & all together contained 128,000,000 cubic feet of Ice'. A couple of days later Cook described passing icebergs 'some of which were near two Miles in circuit and about 200 feet high'.

The ships continued south in sub-zero temperatures, the rigging and sails chequered with ice. On 14 December the horizon was seen to be brighter than usual, with a white reflection visible in the sky. From his experiences in Hudson's Bay, Wales knew before the others that this phenomenon, known as 'the blink of the ice', indicated that they were approaching an ice field. This drawing, which is believed to be by Georg Forster, gives an impression of the way light reflected from the ice in the Antarctic. Cook wrote:

> At half past six we were stoped by an immence field of Ice to
> which we could see no end, over it to the SWBS we thought
> we saw high land, but can by no means assert it. We now
> bore away SSE, SE & SEBS as the Ice trended, keeping close

Georg Forster, 'Ice Islands',
1772—3, gouache (formerly
attributed to William Hodges)   State Library of New South Wales

> Weather and Remarkable Occurrences, towards the South
>
> So that we began to think that we have got into a clear Sea. At about a ¼ past 11 o'Clock We cross'd the Antarctic Circle for at Noon We were by observation four Miles and a half South of it and are undoubtedly the first and only Ship that ever cross'd that line. We now Saw Several Flocks of the Brown and White Pin Tado which We have named Antarctic Petrels because they seem to be natives of that Region; the White Petrel also appear in greater numbers than of late and some few Dark Grey Albatrosses, our constant companions the Blue Petrels have not forsaken us but the Common Pintadoes have quite disapeared as well as many other Sorts which are common in lower Latitudes

by the edge of it, where we saw many Penguins and Whales and many of the Ice Birds, small grey Birds and Pintadoes.

Over the following days the ship remained near the edge of the ice sheet, as Cook searched in vain for a route south. Travel among the icebergs could be extremely dangerous. On 19 December Wales described 'passing continually by very large Islands of Ice which the thickness of the fog hindered us from seeing until we come almost upon them'.

The crew celebrated Christmas among the ice islands. Cook wrote: 'seeing that the People were inclinable to celebrate Christmas Day in their own way, I brought the Sloops under a very snug sail least I should be surprised with a gale [of] wind with a drunken crew'. On New Year's Eve, at 59° south, the ships almost became trapped in the ice when fields closed in from both north and south, receiving 'several hard knocks' before steering clear.

Several days of warmer weather in mid-January allowed the crew, in Cook's words, 'an opportunity to Wash and Dry their Linnen &c a thing that was not a little wanting'. As the wind rose the ships made quick progress in open seas. On 17 January 1773 Cook wrote: 'At about 1/4 past 11 o'Clock we cross'd the Antarctic Circle for at Noon we were by observation four Miles and a half South of it and are undoubtedly the first and only Ship that ever cross'd that line'.

Forster was more emotive, writing that the Antarctic was 'a place where no Navigator ever penetrated, before the British nation, & where few or none will ever penetrate. For it is reserved to the free-spirited sons of Britannia, to navigate the Ocean wherever it spreads its briny waves'.

The ships continued south but soon the horizon began to appear noticeably brighter. At 67° 15′ south Cook wrote: 'The Ice was so thick and close that we could proceed no further':

From the mast head I could see nothing to the Southward but Ice, in the Whole extent from East to WSW without the least appearence of any partition, this immence Field was composed of different kinds of Ice, such as high Hills or Islands, smaller pieces packed close together and what Greenland men properly call field Ice, a piece of this kind, of such extent that I could see no end to it, lay to the SE of us, it was 16 or 18 feet high at least and appeared of a pretty equal height.

Although Cook could not know this, they were only 75 miles (120 kilometres) from the coast of Antarctica. Forster wrote that 'the *Antarctic* Petrels had left us, when we came near the Ice. But a great many whales were seen on all Quarters near the Ice'. Georg Forster made a series of drawings of the animals observed in the southern oceans, including this one of a petrel.

In early February, as the Antarctic summer began to draw to a close, the ships turned northeast towards New Zealand. The *Adventure*, which had kept up throughout the Antarctic cruise despite being a smaller ship, became separated from her companion vessel in fog. The *Resolution* continued towards New Zealand, encountering no land on the way. On 15 March, Forster, beset by the cold and sea water leaking into his cabin, lamented that 'instead of meeting with any object worthy of our attention, after having circumnavigated very near half the globe, we saw nothing, but water, Ice & sky'.

Procellaria similis

Scurvy

During the voyage, Cook would spend much time experimenting with unfamiliar foods in the hope of preventing scurvy, an illness caused by Vitamin C deficiency. He lost only one man through illness during three years at sea and his account of how he did this, including regular cleaning of the ship and remedies such as malt and sauerkraut, was later published in the journal of the Royal Society, becoming a defining text on the subject and winning him the Society's Copley Medal. Cook's success in warding off the disease led to his ideas being widely adopted, although we now know many of the foods he used on the voyage contain little Vitamin C.

In 1753 the naval surgeon James Lind had published *A Treatise of the Scurvy*, in which he described what is often cited as the first modern clinical trial. This had taken place on board HMS *Salisbury* in 1747. He chose twelve patients, each with similar symptoms, and divided them into pairs. Each pair was given a different food or drink, which, based on his reading, he understood to be a commonly proposed remedy. All twelve men were otherwise treated identically. Lind wrote that 'the most sudden and visible good effects were perceived from the use of oranges and lemons'. That lemon juice was not adopted by the Navy until 1795, after which it proved effective in preventing scurvy, is often cited as one of the great failings of medicine.

It was not until 1928 that Vitamin C was identified and its role in preventing scurvy understood. In the eighteenth century the validity of a remedy, and the willingness of the patient to take it, was often judged on how it tasted. The case of Joseph Banks illustrates this. He took with him on the *Endeavour* an 'Essence of Lemon Juice' prepared by Nathaniel Hulme, an Edinburgh doctor who had published a treatise on scurvy in 1768. Banks wrote that on being taken this 'prov'd perfectly good, little if at all inferior in taste to fresh lemon juice'.

123

The Properties of Ice

On the journey south from Plymouth, Cook and Forster had tested an apparatus invented by Charles Irwin to distil fresh water from sea water, something that would be needed if the ships were to undertake a long journey in the Antarctic. On one occasion thirty-one gallons of fresh water were collected over an eleven-hour period. Experiments were also undertaken using thermometers to record the temperature of water at different depths in the ocean.

Despite water rationing and the work of the distilling machine, the allowance of fresh water had been reduced to a pint a day at the end of December. It was known that icebergs in the northern hemisphere contained fresh water and on 9 January boats were launched to collect loose ice, as depicted in this drawing by Hodges. After being warmed in copper pots the ice yielded fifteen tons of fresh water. This solved what would otherwise have been a serious problem. Cook wrote that 'the Melting of the Ice is a little tideous and takes up some time, otherwise this is the most expeditious way of Watering I ever met with'. He continued, 'Experiments are wanting to know what effect cold has on Sea Water … does it freeze or does it not? If it does, what degree of cold is necessary and what becomes of the Salt brine?'

On 14 January, with the ship becalmed near the polar ice sheet, a thermometer was lowered to a hundred fathoms and a temperature of 32° Fahrenheit (freezing point) recorded even though the sea was not frozen. Ice was melted in a pot to test the theory that it 'contained more water than its bulk'. Forster noted instead that the water level reduced and speculated that 'one might be induced to believe, that cold is a real Substance which enters the water & expands it, whilst it is formed into Ice, & which is again expelled by the Fire'. Observing the icebergs as they floated past, he deduced that they were formed on land from snowfall since even the larger ones 'were however all formed of Strata of 4, 5 or 6 Inches high'.

In late February 1773 Cook wrote of the icebergs that:

Great as these dangers are, they are now become so very familiar to us that the apprehensions they cause are never of long duration and are in some measure compencated by the very curious and romantick Views many of these Islands exhibit and which are greatly heightned by the foaming and dashing of the waves against them and into the several holes and caverns which are formed in the most of them, in short the whole exhibits a View which can only be described by the pencle of an able painter and at once fills the mind with admiration and horror.

William Hodges 'The Resolution
& Adventure Taking in Ice for
Water. Lat 61S', 1773
State Library of New South Wales

The First Pacific Circuit

New Zealand

In late March 1773 the *Resolution* arrived off New Zealand and anchored in a deep bay on the mountainous southwest coast of the South Island. Dusky Sound, as Cook called it, proved to be thickly wooded, with waters full of fish. It was autumn in the southern hemisphere and rain fell heavily during the visit. Forster wrote of his first trip ashore: 'The whole Rocks are thick covered with a loose mould & verdure of various kinds: This makes bad walking in the woods, for the rotten trees, the wet moss & the frequent climbers & thick branches of the trees & many more Obstacles hinder you very much'.

The Sound was hemmed in by mountains and was home to only a small number of people. On the first day a group in a canoe approached the ship, stopping three hundred yards away where, according to Wales, 'they lay and viewed her with utmost (seeming) surprise … the Capt. ordered all the People to keep below, and then did all he could to entice them to come nearer, but to no purpose: for when they had satisfied their own

Curiosity, they put about, and returned the way they came'.

A week later one of the boats was hailed from the shore by a man standing on a rock. Cook wrote that 'the man seemed rather afraid when we approached the Rock with our Boat, he however stood firm'. Cook presented him with gifts of handkerchiefs and paper and, in Forster's words, 'shook hands with him, & lastly went up to him & nosed him, which is the mark of friendship among these people'. Two women joined them and they spent 'about half an hour in chitchat which was little understood on either side, in which the youngest of the two Women bore by far the greatest share'.

The visitors and the family got to know each other over the following weeks. The father and eldest daughter, in particular, were regular visitors and became popular with officers and crew. Wales described how during a visit to the landing site the girl befriended a young man her age among the crew:

opposite
Engraving by Daniel Lerpinière, after William Hodges, 'A Family in Dusky Bay, New Zeland', 1776. Versions of this engraving and others reproduced in this chapter were published in James Cook, *A Voyage towards the South Pole and Round the World, performed in His Majesty's Ships the Resolution and Adventure, in the years, 1772, 1773, 1774, and 1775*, 1777
British Library, Add MS 23920, f. 53

right
Engraving after William Hodges, 'Woman of New Zealand', 1776
British Library, Add MS 23920, f. 58

But on his offering at some familliarities, to which I suppose he was emboldened by her apparent fondness, she left him, went and sat down between her father & mother, & I never saw her take the least notice of him afterwards except when one of the Officers offered to shoot him for the insult offered to her, and then she seemed much affected and even shed Tears.

During the stay Cook exchanged gifts with the father, including European tools and clothing, and also left goats and pigs at the Sound to provide a breeding stock of British farm animals. Hodges made sketches of the family and on his return to London worked up a series of oil paintings of Dusky Bay, each of which show the people he met there. The style has been described as both romantic and picturesque, using natural features such as the woods, the deep waters and a waterfall to suggest a remote Arcadia.

After leaving Dusky Sound the *Resolution* sailed north to Queen Charlotte Sound, where the *Adventure* had arrived several weeks before. The landing site became the centre of trade during the stay, with people coming from the North Island to exchange goods with the visitors. The crews of both ships were often asked about Tupaia. Cook, noting that he recognised nobody from the time of the *Endeavour*'s visit, wrote: 'The Name of Tupia was at that time so popular among them that it would be no wonder if at this time it is known over the great part of New Zealand, the name of Tupia may be as familiar to those who never saw him as to those who did'.

During the drunken celebrations of George III's birthday Forster described women being brought on board ship by some of the local men: 'As soon as our young Gentlemen could come up to the price the men set on their favours, they easily yielded them up'. Both Cook and Forster wrote emotionally of what

appeared to be the development of organised prostitution during the stay at the Sound. Cook, who seems to have felt powerless to intervene, wrote:

such are the consequences of a commerce with Europeans and what is still more to our Shame civilized Christians, we debauch their Morals already too prone to vice and we interduce among them wants and perhaps diseases which they never before knew and which serves only to disturb that happy tranquillity they and their fore Fathers had injoy'd. If any one denies the truth of this assertion let him tell me what the Natives of the whole extent of America have gained by the commerce they have had with Europeans.

This is one of the few strongly emotional passages in Cook's journal and illustrates his discomfort at the negative impact of his visit. The idea that the effects of trade were positive and, through spreading wealth, benefited all parties, was a strong element in the thinking of the British about their role in the world. The scenes at Queen Charlotte Sound, in challenging the view of commerce as a benign and 'civilising' force, seem to have been genuinely shocking to Cook, Forster and others who witnessed them.

Drawn from Nature by W. Hodges.

Engraved by J. Caldwall.

O M A I.

Published Feb.ʳ 1ˢᵗ 1777, by Wᵐ. Straban, New Street, Shoe Lane, & Thoˢ. Cadell, in the Strand, London.

Engraving by J. Caldwall, after
William Hodges, 'Omai', 1777
British Library, Add MS 23921, f. 44

Return to Tahiti

On 7 June 1773 the ships left New Zealand and sailed east on a track ten degrees south of the course of the *Endeavour*. After a month in which no land was sighted, Cook turned the ships north in search of Pitcairn Island, which had been sighted by Philip Carteret in 1767, but saw 'no thing excepting two Tropick birds'. Of the Great Southern Continent he wrote: 'Circumstances seem to point out to us that there is none but this is too important a point to be left to conjector, facts must determine it and these can only be had by viseting the remaining unexplored parts of this Sea which will be the work of the remaining part of this Voyage'.

The ships arrived at Tahiti in August 1773. Since the *Endeavour*'s visit a war between rival factions had led to the death of Tuteha and others Cook had known. Richard Pickersgill, on an expedition along the coast, met Purea and found her 'much altered for the worse, poor and of little concequence'. The two leading chiefs were now Vehiatua, a young man who had recently become chief of the area around Vaitepiha Bay following the death of his father, and Tuteha's nephew, Tu, who was chief of the area surrounding Matavai Bay.

Visits to the island by European ships were becoming more common, as was travel by islanders to foreign lands on European ships. Early in the visit excitement was caused when some of the crew reported seeing 'an European who ran directly from them into the Woods … and by his appearance they judged him to be a Frenchman'. Cook showed a number of European flags to the local people and correctly concluded that a Spanish ship had visited the island since the *Endeavour*'s departure. (The mysterious 'Frenchman' was not seen again.)

William Wales compared his observations on life at Tahiti with the European accounts he had read. He poured cold water on Bougainville's account of the promiscuity of Tahitian women:

> *I have great reason to believe that much the greater part of these admit of no such familiarities, or at least are very carefull to whom they grant them … A stranger who visits England might with equal justice draw the Characters of the Ladies there, from those which he might meet with on board the Ships in Plymouth Sound, at Spithead, or in the Thames; on the Point at Portsmouth, or in the Purlieus of Wapping.*

On 1 September 1773 the *Resolution* and *Adventure* left Tahiti, calling at Huahine and Ra'iatea on the journey west. At Huahine a young man called Mai (known by the British as 'Omai') joined the *Adventure*. Mai would later return to London on the *Adventure*, where he would become a celebrity during his stay. At Ra'iatea Cook took on board a young man called Hitihiti ('Odidee'), who travelled on the *Resolution* when it made its second and third crossings of the Antarctic Circle, before returning to Ra'iatea on the *Resolution*'s second visit in June 1774.

Tonga

From Ra'iatea Cook set a course to the southwest where he believed a group of islands described by Tasman were to be found. On 2 October 1773 the island of 'Eua (called by Tasman 'Middleburg Island') was sighted. As the ship approached shore, Cook wrote, 'two Canoes, each conducted by two or 3 men came along side and some of the people into the Ship without the least hesitation, this mark of confidence gave me a good opinion of these Islanders and determined me to anchor'. A chief called Taione ('Tioonee') accompanied the party ashore where they were greeted 'by acclamations from an immence crowd of Men and Women not one of which had so much as a stick in their hands'.

The warmth of the welcome in the place Cook would later call the Friendly Islands led some on board to believe that they had at last found a genuine Arcadian paradise. Wales wrote:

'From the unsuspicious manner in which they first came on board, we had entertained a notion that the Idea of an Enemy was unknown to them, but on going ashore we found that they had several sorts of very formidable Weapons, such as Clubs and spears made of very hard wood'.

The next day the ships sailed the short distance to Tongatapu, the main island. Cook described people running along the shore, 'some having little white flags in their hands which we took for signs of Peace and answered them by hoisting a St Georges Ensign'. By the time the ship reached anchor there were 'a great number of the Islanders aboard and about the sloops, some coming off in Canoes and others swimming off, bringing little else with them but Cloth and other curiosities'. On landing, they were met by 'an immence crowd of men Women

and children who Welcomed us in the same manner as those of Middleburg'. Charles Clerke described the island as 'neither more nor less than one compleat Garden'.

At Tongatapu, Cook was guided around the island by a man called Otago, whom he had met on landing and who he believed was 'a chief or man of some note'. Cook recorded how, on seeing two images set up in 'a house of Worship' and fearing to 'offend either them or their god', he 'did not so much as touch them' but instead asked if they were images of gods. Otago 'turned them over in the doing of which he handled them as roughly as he would have done any other log of wood, which raised a doubt in me that they were representations of the Divinity'. Still, concerned not to cause offence, Cook placed gifts on the shrine, including 'blue Pebbles, some Medals, Nails and other things which my friend took up and carried away with him'.

Later in the visit Otago introduced him to a more senior chief and later still to 'the King of the whole Island'. When Cook gave the King presents, 'I got not one word from him nor did he so much as turn his head or eyes either to the right or left but sit like a Post stuck in the ground'. Nonetheless, later that day a present was sent from the King, which 'consisted of about 20 baskets containing roasted Bananas, sour bread and yams and a Pig of about twenty pound weight'. Cook usually sought to establish relationships with the most senior figure and the wish to identify a single 'king' or 'queen' was a frequent cause of misunderstandings. At Tonga, where the hierarchy of chiefs was more complicated than in most other places, he consistently failed to understand the nature of the ruling group.

William Hodges,
[A Canoe of Tongatapu], 1774
British Library, Add MS 15743, f. 2

Farthest South

William Hodges,
[The *Resolution* in the
Southern Ocean], 1773–4
State Library of New South Wales

Return to the Antarctic

From Tonga the ships sailed south to New Zealand to prepare for another journey into the Antarctic. During a storm off the east coast of the North Island they became separated, with the *Adventure* putting into Tolaga Bay while the *Resolution* continued to the rendezvous at Queen Charlotte Sound. After waiting three weeks for the *Adventure*, Cook wrote a message for Furneaux and buried it beneath a tree with the words 'look underneath' carved into the trunk. He sailed along the coast firing a gun every half hour in case the *Adventure* was in earshot before giving the order 'to proceed directly to the Southward'. The *Adventure* arrived at Queen Charlotte Sound about a week after the *Resolution* sailed.

During the *Adventure's* stay a group of sailors, who had been sent to a nearby bay to collect celery grass, were killed in a fight with a group of Māori men. When their boat failed to return another boat, commanded by James Burney, the second lieutenant, was sent to investigate. Burney described finding the aftermath of a battle on shore and the remains of some of the boat's crew. After firing shots at a group of men on land, the party returned to the ship. Burney wrote in his journal that he thought the killings had probably been unpremeditated and might 'probably happen from Some quarrel'. Furneaux did not stop to investigate the cause of the violence and the *Adventure* sailed for Britain, arriving on 14 July 1774.

After leaving New Zealand the *Resolution* sailed south and by mid-December was again entering seas marked by sub-zero temperatures and increasing numbers of icebergs. On 15 December Forster wrote, 'We found ourselves quite surrounded by large Ice Islands, & large extensive Ice-Fields & some drift-Ice'. Hitihiti, who described the ice islands as 'white, evil, useless', worked with the Forsters in the great cabin helping them to prepare a Tahitian vocabulary and an account of local customs.

On 21 December 1773 Cook wrote that, amid gale-force winds, thick fog and sleeting rain, 'we came the second time under the Polar Circle and stood to the SE'. Cold and damp enshrouded the ship. Forster described his cabin as 'full of unwholesome effluvia & vapours, everything I touch is moist & mouldy & looks more like a subterraneous mansion for the dead than a habitation for the living'. Cook wrote of conditions on deck: 'Our ropes were like wires, Sails like board or plates of Metal and the Shivers froze fast in the blocks'.

On Christmas Day Wales described 'upwards of 200 Islands of Ice in sight, none of which are less than ye ship's Hull'. The wind had died down, leaving the ship almost becalmed. To Forster the icebergs looked 'like the wrecks of a destroyed world'. The dangers of the Antarctic did not prevent the usual seasonal festivities. He continued: 'Everyone of them [the ice islands] threatens us with impending ruin, if you add our solitary Situation & being surrounded by a parcel of drunken Sailors hollowing & hurraing about us, & peeling our Ears continually with Oaths & Execrations, curses & Dam's it has no distant relation to the Image of hell, drawn by the poets'.

Cook had earlier 'got the ship into as clear a birth as we could where she drifted along with the ice islands'. He noted: 'We were fortunate in two things, continual day light and clear weather, had it been foggy nothing less than a miracle could have kept us clear of them'. The ship gradually made progress north and the ice islands began to reduce in size and number.

Like many on board, Forster hoped they would now turn for Cape Horn and home. On 5 January he complained, in an apparent parody of a real conversation with Cook: 'There are people, who are hardened to all feelings, & will give no ear to the dictates of humanity & reason; false ideas of *virtue & good conduct* are to them, to leave nothing to *chance* & future discoverers, by their *perserverance*; which costs the lives of the poor Sailors or at least their healths'.

Farthest South

On 12 January 1774 Cook ordered the ship south again, where it soon ran into a major storm. Forster wrote:

> I did not sleep all night, my Cabin was now below full of water, & I could not stir without being in water to my Ankles … The Ocean & the winds raged all night. The former had no pacific aspect, & seemed to be displeased with the presumption of a few intruding, curious, roving puny mortals, who come into that part of his dominions where he has been undisturbed ever since the creation; perhaps is he more displeased with their business, of seeing for land, where never any was.

Over the next few days the weather became milder and the ship made good progress in an open sea, crossing the Antarctic Circle for the third time on 26 January. Two days later Forster wrote: 'We have never before been so far South, & God knows how far we shall still go on, if Ice or Land does not stop us, we are in a fair way to go to the pole & take a trip round the world in five minutes'.

The ship continued south but began to pass increasing numbers of icebergs. On 30 January Cook wrote:

> A little after 4 AM we precieved the Clowds to the South near the horizon to be of an unusual Snow white brightness which denounced our approach to field ice, soon after it was seen from the Mast-head and at 8 o'Clock we were close to the edge of it which extended East and West in a streight line far beyond our sight; as appear'd by the brightness of the horizon … The Clowds near the horizon were of a perfect Snow whiteness and were difficult to be distinguished from the Ice hills whose lofty summits reached the Clowds. The outer or Northern edge of this immence Ice field was compose[d] of loose or broken ice so close packed together that nothing could enter it; about a Mile in began the firm ice, in one compact solid boddy and seemed to increase in height as you traced it to the South; In this field we counted Ninety Seven Ice Hills or Mountains, many of them vastly large.

He concluded:

> I whose ambition leads me not only farther than any other man has been before me, but as far as I think it possible for man to go, was not sorry at meeting with this interruption, as it in some measure relieved us from the dangers and hardships, inseparable with the Navigation of the Southern Polar regions. Sence therefore we could not proceed one Inch farther South, no other reason need be assigned for our Tacking and stretching back to the North.

William Hodges,
'Ice Islands', 1773–74
State Library of New South Wales

The Second Pacific Circuit

Henry Roberts and James Cook,
[Chart and Sketches of
Easter Island], 1774
British Library, Add MS 31360, f. 34

Easter Island

After spending the summer in the Antarctic, the officers and crew hoped to go home via the Cape of Good Hope. However, Cook decided to make a further extensive circuit of the South Pacific and to explore the southern reaches of the Atlantic before finally turning for home. Cook's decision to make a further search of the South Pacific was prompted partly by the wish to seek out islands not yet visited by Europeans (there no longer being enough unexplored ocean to conceal a continent) and partly to chart accurately the position of islands previously visited by other expeditions. The latter included 'Easter Island, the situation of which is so variously laid down that I have little hopes of finding'. The first European ships to visit Easter Island were those of Jacob Roggeveen's expedition, which arrived on Easter Day 1722. However, without accurate readings of latitude and longitude, the location of the island remained unknown for a further fifty years. Two Spanish expeditions reached the island in the early 1770s, and when the *Resolution* arrived in March 1774 the islanders were familiar with European visits.

As the *Resolution* approached the shore two men came out in a canoe. They presented a bunch of plaintains and were given medals tied with red ribbons. A party landed and was met by about a hundred men who, in Cook's words, 'gave us no disturbance at landing, on the contrary hardly one had so much as a stick in their hands'. Easter Island was the eastern corner of the Polynesian Triangle and Hitihiti was able to talk to the people. Gifts were given and food was exchanged for nails. The visitors were shown the well, which, in Clerke's words, 'was situate so near the Sea, that it rose and fell regularly with the Tide'. Wales realised that Europeans had visited the island recently when he saw 'one man who had a pretty good European hat on'. Hats were particularly prized on the island and both Hitihiti and Hodges had theirs snatched 'from off [their] head & ran away with'.

This chart is believed to have been drawn by Able Seaman Henry Roberts under Cook's supervision and is one of a number of similar charts of islands visited during the voyage. The coastal profile at the bottom of the page shows the view from the deck of the *Resolution*, including a number of statues on the shoreline. Because Cook had fallen ill on the last stages of the Antarctic cruise and, in Forster's words, had become 'very weak & quite emaciated', Pickersgill led a party to explore the island. Much interest was taken in the origin and purpose of the statues. Forster wrote:

> These pillars stand on a kind of pedestal or stone elevation: in some places these elevations are made of regularly hewn square stones sitting as regularly & as finely as can be done by a Nation even with good tools. In what manner they contrived these structures is incomprehensible to me, for we saw no tools with them … these pillars intimate that the Natives were formerly a more powerfull people, more numerous and better civilized; & they are only the monuments of their former grandeur.

Wales reported stopping for lunch beneath one of the statues, its shade 'being sufficient to shelter all our party, consisting of near 30 persons from the Rays of the sun'. He was sceptical of Roggeveen's account of the people 'paying adoration to them at sunrise' and guessed that they were monuments 'to the Memory of some of their Ancient Chiefs & possibly may mark the places where they were buried'.

After failing to find adequate provisions, Cook decided to leave. He wrote: 'No Nation will ever contend for the honour of the discovery of Easter Island as there is hardly an Island in this sea which affords less refreshments and conveniences for Shiping than it does'. Discussing the mystery of the statues, he commented, 'if the Island was once Inhabited by a race of Giants of 12 feet high as one of the Authors of Roggewein's Voyage tell us, than this wonder ceaseth and gives place to another equally as extraordinary, viz. to know what is become of this race of giants'.

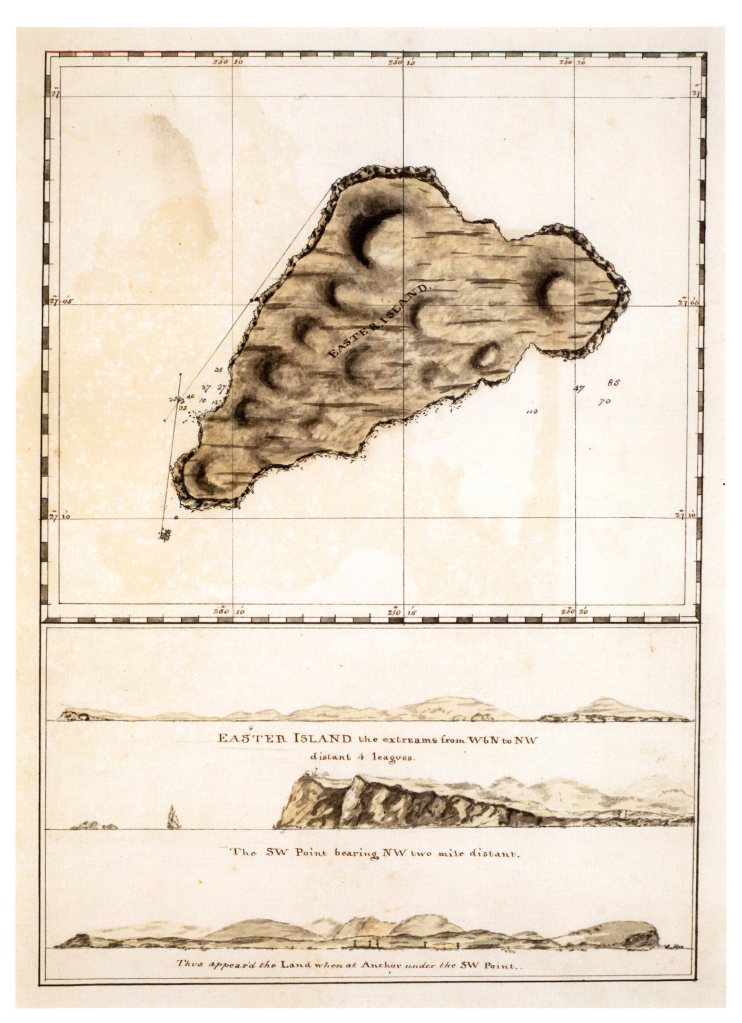

EASTER ISLAND.

EASTER ISLAND the extreams from W b N to NW
distant 4 leagues.

The SW Point bearing NW. two mile distant.

Thus appear'd the Land when at Anchor under the SW Point.

Tu

On 21 April 1774 the *Resolution* arrived again at Tahiti, anchoring at Matavai Bay. Tu visited 'with a vast train and several Chiefs of distinction' bringing a present of ten or twelve hogs. He dined aboard and was presented with gifts. Cook had intended to remain only long enough for Wales to test the chronometer, but on finding a plentiful supply of food and evidence of prosperity in the number of new houses and canoes 'and every other Sign of a riseing state', he decided to stay longer. Forster also noted the country 'in every respect improved', putting the new houses and canoes down 'to the facility they got to build them by the Assistance of our tools of Iron'.

In 1788 Tu would succeed in unifying the various Tahitian chiefdoms into a single kingdom, of which he would, as Pōmare I, be the first king. In 1774 William Wales described him thus:

A Young Man, very tall but slender, and stoops much: He has the appearance of a very stupid Man but His Actions and Government seem to bespeak him a wise active & great Prince … He seems very fond of Millitary Matters: War Canoes are building in every part of his Kingdom; & they had whilst we were here Reviews of one sort or other almost every day.

During the visit Cook ordered the marines to undertake military exercises on the beach, firing repeated musket volleys to the amazement of the onlookers. Tu reciprocated with a mock engagement carried out on the beach by two groups of men armed with spears. Wales noted that Tu 'very good-naturedly, frequently desired us not to be afraid, for that the People would not hurt us'. The ship's cannons were fired at the request of Tu and a display of fireworks was put on.

Before the *Resolution* departed 'the whole Royal Family' came on board the ship and Tu's father presented Cook with a costume of the Chief Mourner. On being shown by Tu 'by far the largest' war canoe being built that he had 'seen at any of the isles', Cook presented him with 'an English Jack and Pendant' and requested that the canoe be named 'Britanne (Brit-annia) the name they have adoped for our Country, to which he very readily consented'.

Tahitian War Canoes

During the stay at Tahiti, Cook, Forster and Hodges went along the coast to Pare to visit Tu. There they found a fleet of war canoes drawn up on the shore, as illustrated by Hodges in this drawing. Cook wrote:

We were surprised when we got there to see upwards of three-hundred of them all rainged in good order for some distance along the Shore all Compleatly equip'd and Man'd, and a vast Crowd of Men on the Shore … We landed however and were received by a Vast Multitude some under Arms and some not, the cry of the latter was Tiyo no Otoo [friend of Tu] and the former Tiyo no Towha [friend of To'ofa], this Cheif as we soon after learnt was General or Admiral of the fleet.

Tu and To'ofa were allies but also rivals. To'ofa took Cook towards his flagship 'where two lines of Arm'd Men were drawn up on the shore before her to keep of the Crowd and clear the way for me'. Cook declined to go aboard and, once back in his own boat, he observed the fleet:

The Cheifs ie all those on the Fighting Stages were drist in their War habits, that is in a vast quantity of Cloth Turbands, breast Plates and Helmmets, some of the latter are of such a length as to greatly incumber the wearer, indeed their whole dress seem'd ill calculated for the day of Battle and seems to be design'd more for shew than use, be this as it may they certainly added grandure to the Prospect,

as they were complesant enough to Shew themselves to the best advantage, their Vessels were decorated with Flags, Streamers &c so that the whole made a grand and Noble appearence such as was never seen before in this Sea.

The next day Tu and Toʻofa visited the *Resolution* for dinner. Forster recorded that the two men 'both told us that the Men of *Morea* & those of *Tiaraboo* were their Ennemies, & desired Capt *Cook* should go with his Ship & fire the Guns against them both'. Cook wrote: 'I made an evasive answer which I believe they understood was not favourable to their request'.

William Hodges, 'War Canoes of Tahiti', 1774–75
British Library, Add MS 15743, f. 8

Engraving by J. Caldwall, after
William Hodges, 'O-Hedidee'
[Hitihiti], 1777
British Library, Add MS 23921, f. 46

Hitihiti

Hitihiti had joined the *Resolution* in September 1773, travelling
to Tonga, New Zealand, the Antarctic and Easter Island. He was
from the island of Bora Bora, the forces of which had occupied
Tupaia's home island of Ra'iatea, and it was at Ra'iatea that he
joined the voyage. Cook wrote that Hitihiti 'says he is a relation
of the great Opoony [Puni] and is a great advocate for Bolabola
of which Island he is a native'. He is believed to have been
seventeen or eighteen years old when he sailed on the *Resolution*.

During the voyage he used a bundle of sticks to help him
memorise the names and locations of new lands, adding to the
knowledge of distant places in the Society Islands. When the
Spanish returned in 1775 they noted names of new islands in the
list of those cited by Tahitian navigators, including 'Pounamu'
(Te Wai Pounamu, the South Island of New Zealand) and
'Fenua Teatea' (which may refer to the North Island). On his
return to Tahiti in 1774 Tu offered him 'lands, honours in short,
everything a king could offer'.

On the day before the ship departed from Tahiti, Cook
wrote that Hitihiti was 'desireous of remaining at this isle' but
that 'every one was persuading him to go with us, telling what
great things he wou'd see and return with immence riches':

*I thought proper to undeceive him, thinking it an Act of
the highest injustice to take away a person from these isles
against his own free inclination under any promise whatever
much more that of bringing them back again, what Man on
board can make such a promise as this. At this time it was
quite un-necessary to persuade any one to go with us, there
were many youths who Voluntary offered themselves to go
with us and even to remain and die in Brit-tania.*

Hitihiti was persuaded to go to Ra'iatea by Forster, who argued
that if he did not return there the people would say 'we killed
Ohediddee & would refuse to give us hogs & provisions'.
Hitihiti decided to remain at Ra'iatea and at his request Cook
wrote a testimonial recommending him 'to the Notice of those
who might come to these isles after me'. He remained on the
ship until it left the harbour and was allowed to fire the
cannons 'for being His Majestys Birth Day we gave them the
Salute at going away'. He then left the ship in a canoe. Wales
wrote that 'when it droped a stern of the ship he gave a look
up at her of unutterable anguish, burst into tears and droped
down in the stern of it'.

The New Hebrides (Vanuatu)

The ship sailed from Ra'iatea in June, calling at Tonga again before continuing west where land was sighted on 17 July 1774. Cook wrote: 'I made no doubt but this was the Australia Del Espiritu Santo of Quiros'. Pedro Fernández de Quirós, convinced that the Southern Continent awaited his discovery, had led an expedition backed by the King of Spain which explored the area in 1606. He landed on Espirito de Santo in present-day Vanuatu, which he believed was part of the continent. Being equally convinced that his mission was to bring Christianity to the peoples of the Pacific, he established a short-lived settlement which he named New Jerusalem. Bougainville had also visited the islands in 1768 on his return from Tahiti.

The chart overleaf shows the course of the *Resolution* as it explored the island group that Cook called the New Hebrides. The seemingly chaotic track of the ship reflects a range of factors, including changeable winds, the search for a landing site with drinking water, and the attempt to chart as much of the coastline of the islands as possible. Each attempt to land drew large crowds to the shore. On 22 July a party landed on the island of Malakula but was discouraged from going inland. Cook decided to leave, taking advantage of the moonlit nights to speed the ship on its journey. On 4 August the *Resolution* arrived off Erromanga, where the landing was initially peaceful, with Cook distributing gifts and being brought water and some coconuts. However, a scuffle broke out around the boats and shots were fired and projectiles, including stones and spears, were thrown. In the violence at least one local man was killed and one of the sailors was wounded.

On 5 August the ship approached the island of Tanna during the night, guided by a large fire burning on it. As dawn broke it became clear that the fire was in fact 'a Volcano which

threw up vast quantaties of fire and smoak'. A landing was made and Cook wrote that there were 'a great number of the islanders assembled in two parties the one on our right and the other on our left, all arm'd with darts, clubs, slings, bows and arrows'. The island was divided into a number of different tribal groups and the division on shore probably reflected this. After distributing gifts to some of the older men Cook ordered two barrels to be filled from a pond to show that this was why he had landed. The ship was moved closer to shore both to speed up the process of taking on board wood and water and as security against attack.

The following morning Cook led a party of marines and sailors in three boats towards the shore, where over a thousand people were assembled, again in two separate groups. Suspecting a trap, he signed for the people on shore to move back and put down their weapons. When this did not happen he ordered musket shots fired over the heads of the crowd on the right but this only prompted a flourishing of weapons and 'one fellow shewed us his back side in such a manner that it was not necessary to have an interpreter to explain his meaning'. Cannon were fired above the crowd from the ship 'which presently dispersed them and then we landed and marked out the limits on the right and [left] by a line'. An old man called Paowang took on the role of intermediary and the people began to return.

William Hodges, 'Mallicolo'
[Malakula], 1774
British Library, Add MS 15743, f. 3

The Entrance of Port Resolution bearing S.S.E. one Mile.

The Entrance of Port Sandwich bearing N.E.W. ½ a mile.

WHITSUNTIDE

Aurora

Lepers Island.

AMBRRYM.

AHPEE

Montague

Hinchinbrook

SANDWICH ISLAND

Ships Track

MALICOLA.

ESPIRITA SANCTO

Bay of St Philip and St James

left
Attrib. Joseph
Gilbert and John
Elliott, [Chart of
Vanuatu with four
views], 1774
British Library,
Add MS 15500, f. 17

right
Engraving by James
Basire, after William
Hodges, 'Woman of
the Island of Tanna'
British Library,
Add MS 23920, f. 90

The ship stayed at Tanna for two weeks. Wales commented that the people 'were in general very quiet and good natured, giving us any thing they had except their Arms, which they refused to part with but for ours, which I thought but reasonable'. Cook reflected on the picture he and his men presented to the inhabitants of the places they visited:

> Its impossible for them to know our real design, we enter their Ports without their daring to make opposition, we attempt to land in a peaceable manner, if this succeeds its well, if not we land nevertheless and mentain the footing we thus got by the Superiority of our fire arms, in what other light can they than at first look upon us but as invaders of their Country; time and some acquaintance with us can only convince them of their mistake.

The engraving above, which is based on an original portrait by William Hodges, shows an unnamed woman from the island, carrying a child. Forster wrote:

> The Women have all the same ornaments as Men, Nose-Stones, Earrings, Shells on the Breast & Bracelets … their heads covered with a kind of cap made of a Plantain leaf or a Mat-Basket. Few are uncovered, & even very young Girls have these Caps. The women carry their young Children on their backs in a kind of bag made of a piece of cloth of the abovementioned kind.

From New Caledonia to New Zealand

In early September the ship arrived at an island that Cook called New Caledonia. So far as is known the *Resolution* was the first European ship to visit. Wales described how as the ship approached the shore people came out in canoes 'seemingly wraped in astonishment … and as soon as we were past them, they all up with their sails & followed us so that (to illustrate small things by large ones) we seemed like a Man-of-War, with a large fleet of Merchantmen under Convoy'. Gifts of Tahitian cloth were lowered from the ship and soon friendly relations were established.

This panoramic work by Hodges shows some of the boats of the island. Wales wrote that 'their Canoes, are all double, with a very heavy Platform over both, on which they have a fire hearth, & generally a fire burning … They do not Paddle, as all the other Nations in these seas do, but work them with large Oars, which pass through holes in the Platform'.

After leaving New Caledonia, the ship sailed back to New Zealand, calling on the way at an uninhabited island, which Cook called Norfolk Island. When the *Resolution* arrived at Queen Charlotte Sound in October 1774 it was several days before contact was made with the local people. Although the British were still unaware of the incident, it seems likely that the inhabitants of the Sound feared retribution for the deaths of the men from the *Adventure*. Forster described the approach of two canoes: 'They had their Sails up, but when they saw the Ship, down came the Sail & they paddled back as fast as possible'. Cook wrote that the people had 'taken to the Woods and hills', but on re-establishing contact 'they knew us again, joy took the place of fear, they hurried out of the woods, embraced us over and over and skiped about like Mad men'.

William Hodges, [View of Balade
Harbour, New Caledonia], 1774
British Library, Add MS 15743, f. 10

Completing the Search of the
Southern Oceans

The *Resolution* left Queen Charlotte Sound on 10 November 1774. Cook steered southeast, intending to cross the Pacific on the 54th or 55th parallel 'so as to pass over those parts which were left unexplored last summer'. On 28 November Forster wrote: 'We advance amazingly on the pinions of the swiftest gales'. No land was found on the passage across the Pacific. On 17 December the west coast of Tierra del Fuego was sighted. Cook wrote: 'I have now done with the SOUTHERN PACIFIC OCEAN, and flatter my self that no one will think that I have left it unexplor'd, or that more could have been done in one voyage towards obtaining that end than has been done in this'.

For the first time in three years Christmas was celebrated in harbour. A large number of geese were shot and Cook wrote:

'Roast and boiled Geese, Goose pies &c was victuals little known to us, and we had yet some Madeira wine left … our friends in England did not perhaps, celebrate Christmas more cheerfully'. Forster, however, complained: 'We were disturbed during night by our Ships-Crew, who allmost all got drunk in honor of the Christmass-day'.

The *Resolution* rounded Cape Horn on 29 December and continued east into the Atlantic in search of a coastline shown in a map drawn by Alexander Dalrymple, a leading advocate of the existence of the Great Southern Continent. Cook doubted the coastline's existence and was not unhappy when, having explored the area, he was able to record 'neither land nor signs of any'. The ship continued east and on 15 January 1775 an island was sighted. Approaching the shore in one of the boats,

Cook described towering cliffs covered 'by a huge Mass of Snow and ice of vast extent':

> Pieces were continually breaking from them and floating out to sea. A great fall happened while we were in the Bay; it made a noise like Cannon. The inner parts of the Country was not less savage and horrible: the Wild rocks raised their lofty summits till they were lost in the Clouds and the Vallies laid buried in everlasting Snow.

Sailing further south, the ship arrived at a group of small islands, one of which was named Freezland Rock after the sailor who first sighted it. The southernmost island was named Southern

'Chart of the Southern
hemisphere Shewing the
Track and Discoveries made
by the Resolution under the
command of Captain Cook'
British Library, Add MS 31360, f. 7

Thule at Forster's suggestion, denoting that it marked the edge of the known world.

Opinions had varied throughout the voyage on whether ice was formed on land or at sea, but the discovery of South Georgia and the South Sandwich Islands provided clear illustrations of ice being formed on land. In Clerke's words, the 'sight of those Lands at the bottom of the Atlantic render'd this matter very plain'. Cook wrote:

> I concluded that what we had seen, which I named Sandwich Land was either a group of Islands or else a point of the Continent, for I firmly beleive that there is a tract of land near the Pole, which is the Source of most of the ice which is spread over this vast Southern Ocean: and I think it also probable that it extends farthest to the North opposite the Southern Atlantick and Indian Oceans because ice has always been found farther to the north in these Oceans than anywhere else, which, I think, could not be if there was no land to the South.

He concluded: 'The risk one runs in exploreing a coast in these unknown and Icy Seas, is so very great, that I can be bold to say, that no man will ever venture farther than I have done and that the lands which may lie to the South will never be explored'. On Forster's advice, Hodges added the figures of '*Labour* & *Science*

supporting the Globe' to the map 'representing the Southern Hemisphere & our Ships track on it'.

The *Resolution* continued east across the Atlantic until it was directly south of the coast of Africa. Cook wrote:

> I had now made the circuit of the Southern Ocean in a high Latitude and traversed it in such a manner as to leave not the least room for the Possibility of there being a continent, unless near the Pole and out of the reach of Navigation … By twice visiting the Pacific Tropical Sea, I had not only settled the situation of some old discoveries but made there many new ones and left, I conceive, very little more to be done even in that part. Thus I flater my self that the intention of the Voyage has in every respect been fully Answered, the Southern Hemisphere sufficiently explored and a final end put to the searching after a Southern Continent.

He decided to sail for the Cape of Good Hope, writing that 'our sails and rigging were so much worn that some thing was giving way every hour and we had nothing left either to repair or replace them'. On arrival it was discovered that by going round the world in an easterly direction 'we had gained a day'. The *Resolution* stayed a month at the Cape before returning home via St Helena, Ascension Island and the Azores.

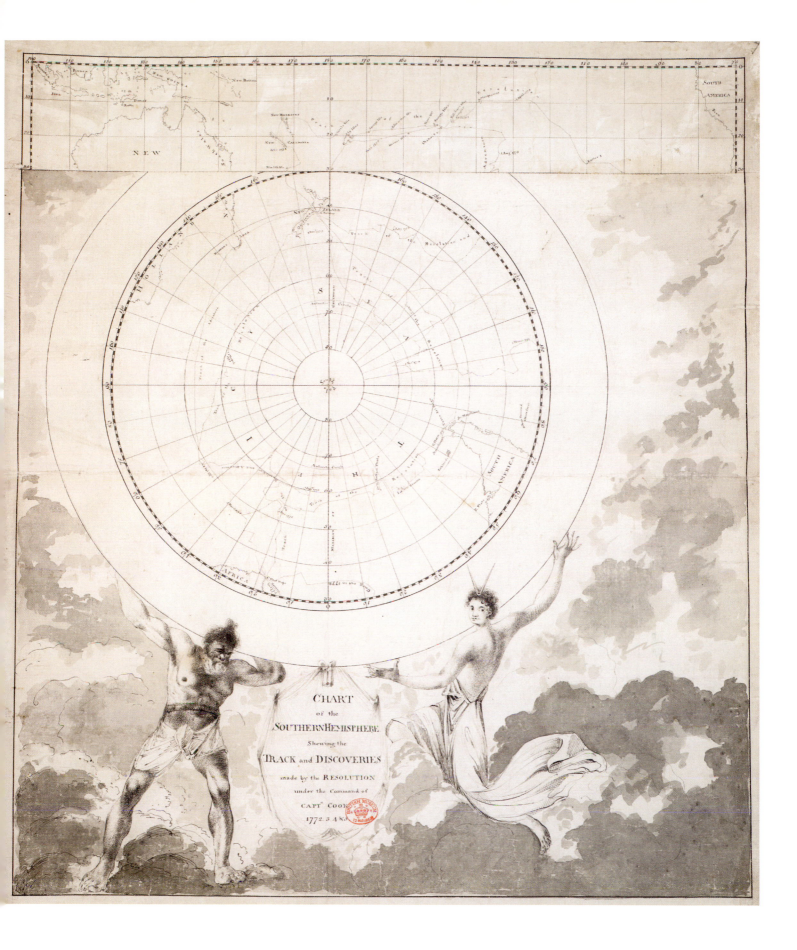

CHART
of the
SOUTHERN HEMISPHERE
Shewing the
TRACK and DISCOVERIES
made by the RESOLUTION
under the Command of
CAPT COOK
1772. 3 4 &

BETWEEN THE VOYAGES (1774–76)
'Noble Savages' and the Northwest Passage

The *Adventure* had returned to Britain in July 1774, a year ahead of the *Resolution*. Furneaux's decision to sail home from New Zealand meant that Mai ('Omai'), who had joined the voyage at Ra'iatea, remained on board. He was the first Polynesian to visit Britain, and on his arrival in London Joseph Banks and the Earl of Sandwich effectively became his guardians. The two men, aware of the deaths of three Inuit people who had recently visited London, arranged for him to be inoculated against smallpox. Mai lived for a time with Banks in his London house, where he was tutored in the ways of society. Banks took him to Kew to meet the Royal Family. He dined with the Royal Society and was taken to Cambridge to meet a group of the country's leading scholars. He attended the opening of the House of Lords, where George III lambasted the American colonists, then in revolt, for their disloyalty.

During his time in Britain Mai became a symbol of the simpler and more innocent life that was believed by many to exist in the islands of the Pacific. At a weekend party at Sandwich's country estate he cooked mutton for the guests in the traditional Tahitian way, wrapping the meat in leaves and placing it in the ground on heated stones. Joshua Reynolds painted him, dressed in white robes, against a backdrop of a tropical island at night, evoking both purity and mystery. In William Parry's painting he is again shown dressed in flowing white robes, with Banks (standing) and Solander (seated). Fanny Burney, whose brother James was second lieutenant on the *Adventure*, described him as 'lively and intelligent, and seems so open and frank-hearted, that he looks every one in the face as his friend and well-wisher'.

London during this period was witnessing a rapid growth in its consumer economy. The *Oxford English Dictionary* cites the first known use of the verb 'to shop' as 1764. Luxury goods previously only available to the wealthy were becoming increasingly accessible to a growing middle class, epitomised by Josiah Wedgwood's pottery made in his works at Etruria. In her 1778 novel *Evelina*, Fanny Burney describes the social round of middle-class life in London. Like Mai, Evelina is a newcomer to London. She is pitched headlong into the social whirl, where she finds that 'many things are unaccountable and perplexing'. She takes part in the new activity of 'seeing sights', including the pleasure gardens at Ranelagh and Vauxhall, a mechanical museum, auctions (where the property of bankrupts is sold off), the theatre and the opera. Visits to a hairdresser ('you can't think how oddly my head feels; full of powder and black pins, and a great cushion on top of it') and haberdashers ('I should never have chosen a silk, for they produced so many I knew not which to fix upon, and they recommended them all so strongly') mark her entry into the world.

The question of the extent to which Mai's behaviour was 'natural' or the result of coaching by Banks was much debated. Samuel Johnson admitted to being struck by 'the elegance of [Mai's] behaviour' but argued that this was because he had 'passed his time, while in England, only in the best company; so that all that he had acquired of our manners was genteel'. The author of an anonymous poem entitled 'An Historic Epistle from Omiah [Mai] to the Queen of Otaheite [Purea]' taunted Banks, describing the poem as a 'plant of your growth' and noting: 'I have ordered the original manuscript to be left at the printer's (after the manner of Ossian's) as an incontestable proof that it could only be written by Omiah himself'. The poem begins:

> *To thee, Great Queen! whom happier realms obey,*
> *OMIAH sends this tributary lay;*
> *Him, far from comfort, Fate's decrees have hurl'd,*
> *A wand'ring vagrant in the northern world;*
> *A world of prejudice, where Error rules,*
> *By Folly bred, and rear'd in Fashion's schools;*

Where on a gilded car in state she rides,
Whilst custom draws, and ignorance misguides,
Where strange pursuits the mad'ning croud engage,
Where book worms plod, and system builders rage.

Against the backdrop of an increasingly sophisticated metropolitan culture, the idea of the 'noble savage' was a powerful one for eighteenth-century audiences. The outsider, typically someone from an unfamiliar culture, was characterised as naturally simple and good, highlighting the supposedly artificial and corrupting nature of modern European life. The idea is particularly associated with the views of Rousseau, although it in fact has a long history in European thought. The anonymous poem cited above goes on to contrast the patriotic belief in the British nature of liberty with the allegedly brutal actions of the British abroad, again using the fiction that it is describing the world through Mai's eyes:

Yet in cool blood premeditately go
To murder wretches whom they cannot know.
Urg'd by no inj'ry, prompted by no ill,
In forms they butcher, and by systems kill;
Crossed o'er the seas, to ravage distant realms,
And ruin thousands worthier than themselves.
Methinks, you ask, what wondrous wealth can bribe
The liberal mind to join this hateful tribe?

When the *Resolution* returned to Britain in summer 1775 Mai was accompanying Sandwich, Banks and Martha Ray, Sandwich's mistress, on a tour of the naval dockyards of the south coast, including an inspection of HMS *Victory*. By this time his celebrity had started to fade and he was living alone in lodgings in Warwick Street. Concerns were being raised as to his long-term future.

Following the controversies over Hawkesworth's book, the Admiralty was well aware of the risk that the return of Cook's second voyage would lead to controversy. It was agreed that the official account would be published in two volumes, the first a narrative of events written by Cook and the second an account of the scientific observations by Forster. John Douglas, Canon of Windsor, was chosen to assist Cook in preparing his book. Cook was also keenly aware of the sensational nature of the stories that had circulated in London after the return of the *Endeavour* and an initial concern was that the book should not fan these flames. In January 1776 he wrote to Douglas:

With respect to the amours of my people at Otaheite & other
places I think it will not be necessary to mention them at all
unless it will be by way of throwing a light on the character
or the customs of the People we were then among; and even
then I would have it done in such a manner as might be
unexceptionable to the nicest reader. In short my desire is
that nothing indecent may appear in the whole book, and
you cannot oblige me more than by painting out whatever
may appear to you as such.

The poor relationship with Forster, which had bedevilled the voyage, continued in London. In June 1776 Cook reported that he had failed to turn up for a meeting: 'I suppose he will publish as soon as possible and if so he will get the start of me. He has quite deceived me … but it cannot hurt me & I am only sorry my Lord Sandwich has taken so much trouble to serve an undeserving man.' Although Forster was prevented from publishing his account by his contract with the Admiralty, his son, Georg, was able to publish ahead of Cook. The book contained a range of criticisms of Cook and others on the voyage, including allegations of wanton violence and sexual exploitation, plus a Rousseau-like attack on the impact of Europeans in visiting remote places:

> It were indeed sincerely to be wished, that the intercourse which has lately subsisted between Europeans and the natives of the South Sea islands may be broken off in time, before the corruption of manners, which unhappily characterises civilized regions, may reach that innocent race of men, who live here fortunate in their ignorance and simplicity.

In this context an interesting account of Mai's views on British morality survives. The anti-slavery campaigner Granville Sharp later recalled a conversation in which he tried to teach the tenets of Christianity to Mai, and in particular to recommend monogamy. Mai, with the example of the Earl of Sandwich in mind, was puzzled by the application of sexual morality in Britain. He used three pens to explain this to Sharp:

> 'There lies Lord S-----' (a Nobleman with whom he was well acquainted, and in whose family he had spent some time); and then he took another pen, and laid it close by the side of the former pen, saying, 'and there lies Miss W-----' (who was

an accomplished young woman in many respects, but, unhappily for herself, she lived in a state of adultery with that nobleman); and then he took a third pen, and placing it on the table at a considerable distance from the other two pens … in a pensive posture, he said, 'and there lie Lady S-----, and cry!'

The Earl of Sandwich was one of the key figures in organising Cook's third voyage. On his return to London Cook had planned to retire from active service and had accepted a position at the Royal Hospital, Greenwich. However, astute management by Sandwich of a meeting that Cook attended as an advisor prompted him to volunteer to lead a third expedition, this time to explore the North Pacific and search for a passage from there to the Atlantic. To conceal the real purpose from rival European powers, the voyage was presented publicly as a humanitarian mission to return Mai to his homeland.

A navigable northern passage between Atlantic and Pacific had been a dream of British strategists since the sixteenth century, both to shorten the journey to the Pacific and as a trade route free from the interference of foreign powers. An expedition led by John Byron had been sent to the Pacific in search of the Passage by the Admiralty in 1765. As perhaps befitted the grandfather of the poet, Byron had ignored his orders to sail north up the coast of the Americas and, instead, sailed west in search of the Solomon Islands and their fabled riches. In 1773, following prompting from Joseph Banks, Daines Barrington and the Royal Society, the Admiralty had sent two ships, HMS *Racehorse* and HMS *Carcass*, north to the Arctic, where they had run into an impenetrable ice barrier near Spitsbergen in the Barents Sea.

In 1774 a book entitled *An Account of the New Northern Archipelago, Lately Discovered by the Russians in the Seas of Kamtschatka and Anadir* was published in London. This was a translation of a work by Jacob von Staehlin, Secretary to the Imperial Academy of Sciences in St Petersburg. It included a map showing a large group of islands in the North Pacific and highlighted the potential of the fur trade there. Perhaps prompted by this, Daines Barrington called for a further British expedition to search for a passage from the Atlantic to the Pacific. In 1775 he published a long pamphlet entitled *The Probability of Reaching the North Pole Discussed*, which argued for the existence of an open polar sea. Mixing scientific, economic and theological arguments, he extrapolated the conclusion that there was open sea around the North Pole, which would allow safe passage across the roof of the world. The pamphlet emphasised the commercial advantages of discovering islands to the north and a passage between Atlantic and Pacific:

> *The benefits derived from these discoveries, and the commerce arising from them, will necessarily extend to all parts of our dominions. For however fit the poor people of those islands may be for such enterprises, or however commodious the ports in their countries may be found for equipping and receiving vessels employed in these voyages, yet the commodities, manufactures, &c. must be furnished from all parts of the British empire, and of course be of universal advantage.*

This came at a time when new technological processes were beginning to change the nature of industry in Britain. In 1775 Matthew Boulton and James Watt formed their partnership, which brought together the mass-production methods of Boulton's Birmingham factory and Watt's revolutionary new design for a more efficient steam engine. The use of steam power to drive machines would lead to vast changes in production methods over the following decades, opening the way to trade on a scale that would have been unimaginable to previous generations. Adam Smith's book, *An Inquiry into the Nature and Causes of the Wealth of Nations*, which argued for the benefits of free trade, was published in March 1776. For Smith, free trade allowed the 'mutual communication of knowledge and of all sorts of improvements which an extensive commerce from all countries to all countries naturally, or rather necessarily, carries along with it'. Smith identified the division of labour, which allowed economies of scale, as the critical development in modern industry.

Cook's third voyage left Britain in July 1776, with the task of exploring and charting the coasts of the North Pacific, the only major area of inhabited coastline remaining to be surveyed and represented on European maps. If Cook's voyages have a symbolic importance as the point at which the map of the world, at least in rough outline, moved close to completion, the development of Watt's steam engine and the publication of *The Wealth of Nations* were perhaps equally symbolic of the beginnings of globalisation.

John Cleveley Jr,
*Racehorse and Carcass
Trapped in Ice near
Spitsbergen, 1773*. Plate LVI in
Basil Lubbock, *Adventures by
sea from art of old time* (1925).
British Library, 7854.v.21

those who could not
they dashed their bra
advanced a few paces
fired, the Stones flew
the Lieut down & a
him in the back wi
himself shot the In
the water. Captain
on the Rock, he was
the Pinnace, holdin
Back of his head
carrying his mus
An Indian came
once or twice as he

THE THIRD VOYAGE

1776–80

The Instructions

Cook's third voyage was as ambitious in its object as the previous two voyages. The Admiralty's instructions stipulated that he was to sail via Tahiti to the west coast of North America (known by the British as 'New Albion') where, above 65° north, he was to 'explore such Rivers or Inlets as may appear to be of considerable extent and pointing towards Hudsons or Baffins Bay'. The Admiralty recognised the coastline further south as Spanish territory and Cook was instructed 'to be very careful not to give any umbrage or offence to any of the Inhabitants or Subjects of His Catholic Majesty'.

If he failed to find the passage he was to winter in the Russian port of Petropavlovsk on the Kamchatka peninsula 'or wherever else you shall judge more proper'. The following spring he was to 'proceed from thence to the Northward as far as, in your prudence, you may think proper, in further search of a North East, or North West passage, from the Pacific Ocean into the Atlantic Ocean, or the North Sea'. There were similar instructions to those for earlier voyages on surveying unfamiliar lands, relationships with the peoples visited, and the circumstances in which inhabited and uninhabited land should be claimed for the British Crown. Cook was given an Inuit dictionary compiled on the east coast, in case the people of the west coast spoke the same language.

Cook took command of the *Resolution,* and John Gore, who had sailed on the *Endeavour,* was commissioned as first lieutenant. William Bligh, who would later become famous as the captain of the *Bounty,* was appointed as master. The second ship was the *Discovery,* also a Whitby collier, captained by Charles Clerke. James Burney, who had sailed on the *Adventure,* was the first lieutenant and George Vancouver, who would later chart much of the west coast of Canada, was one of the mid-shipmen. Perhaps because of the dispute with the Forsters, no high-profile civilian scientists were recruited. David Nelson, an employee of Kew Gardens, was appointed to collect plant specimens. William Bayly was appointed as astronomer on the *Resolution,* while William Anderson, the surgeon, and James King, the second lieutenant, both had some scientific training.

On his previous voyages Cook had attempted to transplant European crops and animals to the places he visited. This was intended to provide supplies for future expeditions, but also had the loftier goal of bringing the benefits of British agriculture to the Pacific. On this voyage, backed by the enthusiasm generated by Mai's visit, the ambition was much greater. On 10 June the *Resolution* 'took on board a bull, 2 cows with their calves and some sheep to carry to Otaheite with a quantity of Hay and Corn for their subsistence. These cattle were put on board at his Majesty's Command and expence'. At Cape Town more animals, including cattle and horses, were purchased.

The *Resolution* sailed in search of the Northwest Passage on 12 July 1776, almost exactly four years after it had sailed in search of the Great Southern Continent. Distracted by his publishing deadline and the dispute with the Forsters, Cook did not oversee the repairs to the ships in the same detail as he had done on his two previous voyages. Rotten wood was used in some of the repairs and the caulking (sealing of gaps in the ship to make it watertight) was inadequate. The poor state of the ships was not discovered until after they had left Britain. To add to the problems, Charles Clerke was imprisoned shortly before the ships were due to sail because he had acted as guarantor for his brother's debts. The *Discovery* did not sail until he was released and only caught up with the *Resolution* at Cape Town. During his imprisonment Clerke contracted tuberculosis, of which he would later die.

Nathaniel Dance-Holland,
Charles Clerke, 1776
Government House, Wellington,
New Zealand

Johann Mottet,
Portrait of John Webber,
1812 (after an earlier miniature),
oil on canvas
Bernisches Historisches Museum,
Berne

John Webber,
'A Dance at Otaheite', 1777
British Library, Add MS 15513, f. 19

John Webber

John Webber (1751–1793) was employed by the Admiralty as the expedition's artist. He was the son of Abraham Wäber, a sculptor from Berne who settled in Britain in the 1740s, and Mary Quant, a Londoner. Webber was sent to live with his aunt in Berne in 1757 and in 1767 was apprenticed to Johann Ludwig Aberli, a Swiss topographical artist. In 1770 he went to study in Paris, where he developed his skills in landscape painting. He returned to London in 1775 and enrolled at the Royal Academy Schools, where a year later he exhibited three paintings. These caught the eye of Daniel Solander, who recommended Webber to the Admiralty as the artist for Cook's third voyage.

Webber was instructed to 'make Drawings and Paintings of such places in the Countries you may touch at in the course of the said Voyage as may be proper to give a more perfect Idea thereof than can be formed by written descriptions only'. He worked closely with Cook in recording the voyage, and many of his pictures can be matched to passages in Cook's journal. Webber was later appointed by the Admiralty to create the engravings that would accompany the published account of the voyage. Much of his later career was based on work undertaken on the voyage. He published many prints, aquatints and etchings of Pacific scenes in addition to continuing to work as a landscape painter in Europe.

Cape Town to the Society Islands

Introduction

The ships left the Cape in October 1776. They initially sailed south in search of islands discovered by the French explorer Yves-Joseph de Kerguelen-Trémarec, which the Admiralty had instructed Cook to locate. After a brief landing at the main island, which Cook called the Island of Desolation owing to its bleak appearance, the ships sailed northwest towards New Zealand, stopping briefly at Adventure Bay on the south coast of Tasmania. Furneaux had landed there during the second voyage and had also investigated the northern coast, wrongly concluding that Tasmania was joined to the mainland. Cook seems to have accepted this: 'I hardly need say it is the Southern point of New Holland, which if not a Continent is one of the largest islands in the World.'

The ships arrived at Queen Charlotte Sound in New Zealand in February 1777. David Samwell, the surgeon's mate, described how the ship became a 'second Noahs Ark, [and] poured out the Horses, Cattle, Sheep, Goats &c. with peacocks, Turkeys, Geese & Ducks, to the great Astonishment of the New Zealanders, who had never seen horses or Horned Cattle before'. After a brief stay to take on supplies, during which time Cook also investigated the deaths of the men from the *Adventure* in 1773, the ships sailed north. At Mai's request two young Māori, Te Weherua and Koa, joined the voyage. Cook had intended to sail directly to Tahiti but, because of adverse winds, instead turned towards Tonga.

In March the ships reached the previously unexplored islands of Mangaia and Atiu (now part of the Cook Islands). Stops were also made at the Hervey Islands and Palmerston Island to take on provisions. The ships stayed at Tonga for three months, from May to July 1777, visiting a number of islands including Nomuka, Lifuka, Tongatapu, and 'Eua. At 'Eua Cook presented a ram and two ewes to Taione, the chief who had welcomed him on the second voyage. He climbed a hill and looked down on

John Webber,
'The Wattle Bird', 1777
British Library, Add MS 17277, no. 9

the island spread out below him: 'I could not help flattering myself with the idea that some future navigator may from the very same station behold these meadows stocked with cattle, the English have planted at these islands.' Before leaving he planted some pineapples and 'had a dish of turnips to dinner, being the produce of the seeds I left last voyage'.

The ships anchored at Vaitepiha Bay, Tahiti on 12 August. Canoes came out to trade, bringing news that both Vehiatua and Purea had died. The Spanish had visited since Cook's last visit,

John Webber,
[View of Tahiti], 1777
British Library, Add MS 15513, f. 13

leaving two priests on the island to establish a Catholic mission, which was abandoned after less than a year. They had left hogs, goats, dogs and a bull on the island, which Cook described as 'very fine'. Anderson noted that the Spanish had presented themselves as 'superior to any European nation that have yet visited them. According to the natives they represented the English, who first discovered and oftenest visited the Island, particularly as far inferior to them in power and grandeur'. They had erected a cross on the site of the mission, on which they carved a notice proclaiming their ownership of the island. Cook had this altered to reflect the British claim.

The ships continued to Matavai Bay, where relations were renewed with Tu and To'ofa. Cook brought ashore poultry (including a peacock and hen that Lord Bessborough had given him), cattle, horses and sheep. He wrote that he:

found myself lightened of a very heavy burden, the trouble and vexation that attended the bringing of these animals thus far is hardly to be conceived. But the satisfaction I felt in having been so fortunate as to fulfil His Majesty's design in sending such useful animals to two worthy nations sufficiently recompensed me for the many anxious hours I had on their account.

Most commentators agree that during the third voyage Cook's behaviour became more erratic and some of his responses to thefts harsher. At Tonga he had ordered a chief to be flogged for

stealing, and during the stay in the Society Islands a number of incidents occurred, including the burning of houses and canoes at Mo'orea after a goat was stolen. Although Cook does not mention the incident in his journal, King recorded that a man who was on board the ship from Mo'orea to Huahine was caught stealing and 'the Captain in a Passion orderd the Barber to shave his head & cut off his ears … luckily for the fellows ears, an officer was looking on & stopd the barber, being convinced that the Captn was only in a Passion, & made him go to him to receive fresh orders'. The orders were cancelled and 'the fellow escap'd with the lobe of one ear cut away'.

At Huahine a sextant was stolen and the culprit caught, with Mai's help. Cook mentions in his journal that he ordered a punishment 'of greater severity than I had ever done any one before' but does not say what this entailed. Clerke wrote: 'The extraordinary impudence and audacity of the fellow whilst in confinement on board, surpassed every thing; which determin'd Capt Cook to make a publick and severe example of him, in consequence of which resolution, he was deprived of his Ears and turned on shore'.

These and other incidents have led to fierce historical debates over whether Cook suffered a personality change between the second and third voyage. Some have argued that he was suffering an illness that made him subject to fits of rage, while others have pointed to his use of floggings and hostage-taking as a deterrent against theft on earlier voyages, and have seen his later actions as simply an extension of that behaviour.

'A View of Christmas Harbour'

Following what Clerke described as a 'tedious and dangerous'
detour, the ships arrived at the Kerguelen Islands and a party
landed on the main island on Christmas Day 1776. Cook wrote
that 'every gully afforded a large Stream, but I found not a single
tree or shrub'.

This watercolour by John Webber depicts 'Christmas
Harbour', with the *Resolution* and *Discovery* at anchor. A group
of penguins watch the visitors from the shore, while a seal sleeps
on the beach. Cook wrote: 'I found the shore in a manner
covered with Penguins and other birds and Seals, but these were
not numerous, but so fearless that we killed as ma[n]y as we
chose for the sake of their fat and blubber to make Oil for our
lamps and other uses'.

On 27 December Cook gave the men a day off in lieu of
Christmas Day and many went to explore the island, 'which
they found barren and desolate in the highest degree'. One of
the sailors returned with a message in a bottle, which had been
left during the visit by one of Kerguelen's ships in 1772. Despite
clear evidence that the French had been there before him, Cook
'display'd the British flag and named the harbour Christmas
harbour as we entered it on that Festival'. Anderson described
this as 'a circumstance not only contrary to the law of nations
but if seriously meant to the law of nature as being in itself not
only unjust but truly ridiculous, and perhaps fitter to excite
laughter than indignation'.

The Last Visit to New Zealand

This watercolour depicts a *Pā* or fortified settlement at Queen Charlotte Sound in New Zealand. When the ships arrived in February 1777 many people who were known from previous visits were reluctant to come on board, owing to fear of retribution for the deaths of the men from the *Adventure* in 1773. In July 1772 the French explorer Marion du Fresne and twenty-four of his men had been killed in a dispute in the Bay of Islands. The British certainly knew of this and, although it happened several hundred miles to the north, it is possible that the people of Queen Charlotte Sound had heard news of the French reprisals, which included burning a village and killing an estimated 250 people. Relations on both sides were, therefore, nervous. A side effect was that many of the crew were now scared to sleep with the local women.

On 16 February Cook, Clerke, Mai and several others went to 'Grass Cove', the place where the conflict had occurred. Cook asked Mai to find out from an 'old friend', whom he called Pedro, what had happened at the cove:

> *They told us that while our people were at victuals with several of the natives about them some of the latter stole or snatched from them some bread, & fish for which they were beat this being resented a quarrel insued, in which two of the Natives were shot dead, by the only two Muskets that were fired, for before they had time to discharge a third or load those that were fired they were all seized and knocked on the head.*

Kahura, a Ngāti Kuia and Rangitāne chief, was said by people in the area to be the man responsible. The question of whether or not the attack was premeditated seems to have been critical to Cook's assessment of the killings. At Grass Cove he wrote: 'For Kahoura's greatest enemies, those who solicited his

opposite
John Webber,
'The Hippah', 1777
British Library, Add MS 15513, f. 6

right
John Webber,
'Portrait of Kahura', 1777
State Library of New South Wales

distruction the most, owned that he had no intention to quarrel, much less to kill till the quarrel was actually commenced'. Kahura visited the landing site three times, in Cook's words, 'without shewing the least mark of fear'. On the third occasion Cook invited him on board and later summarised Kahura's account of the cause of the violence, while putting his own interpretation on the story:

On offering a stone hatchet for sale to one of the people, he [the sailor] kept it and would give nothing in return, on which they snatched from them some bread while they were at victuals. The remainder of his account of this unhappy affair differed little from what we had been told by other people, but the story of the Hatchet was certainly invented by Kahourah to make the English appear the first aggressors.

It was while in Cook's cabin that Kahura asked to have his portrait painted and Webber produced this pen and wash drawing. Cook's decision not to take action against Kahura divided his officers and outraged many of his men. Samwell recorded:

Concerning this unfortunate affair we were divided in our Opinions, some laying the whole blame upon the New Zealanders, looking upon it as a concerted Scheme of theirs to cut off our people & that the Man was set on to steal in order to pick a Quarrel with us, while others are inclined to think it was merely accidental & that the New Zealanders were incited to revenge the Death of their Countryman.

John Webber,
[Entertainments at Lifuka
on the reception of
Captain Cook], 1777
British Library, Add MS 15513, f. 8

Entertainments at Lifuka

During much of the three-month period Cook spent in Tonga he was accompanied by a senior chief called Finau, who arrived at Nomuka from Tongatapu in early May and travelled with him to other islands. Although the British believed him to be the king, he was in fact the Tuʻi Kanokopolu, one of the ruling titles of Tonga.

This watercolour was described by Webber as showing 'the manner of receiving, entertaining and making Captain Cook a present of the productions of the Island, on his Arrival'. It shows the reception of Cook at Lifuka in the Haʻapai island group in May 1777. The figure under the canopy at the centre of the painting may be Finau and Cook is probably one of the people next to him. In the centre of the ring of spectators, men are participating in single combat, in which 'if the Challenge was excepted, which was generally the case, each put himself in a proper attitude and began to engage and continued till one or the other gave out or their weapons were broke'. Other men are boxing, which was 'very little different from the method practised in England. But what struck us with the most surprise was to see a couple of lusty wenches step forth and without the least ceremony fall to boxing, and with a[s] much art as the men'.

A couple of days later, on 20 May, the British put on firework displays, music and drills by the marines. Anderson wrote:

They seem'd well pleased with the firing and various motions which were made, though our soldiers were by no means examples of the best discipline. In their turn they exhibited a dance and exercised their clubs, in which it was acknowledg'd by all they far outdid our people in exactness and dexterity.

Cook described the effect of the firework display, which included 'some sky and Water Rockets which astonished and pleased them beyond measure and intirely turned the scale in our favour'.

A Ceremony at Tongatapu

One way in which Cook's role evolved on this voyage was that he began to take a more active part in recording the society, culture and beliefs of the people in the places he visited, something which on the previous voyages would have been primarily the role of Banks or Forster. His journal contains extremely detailed accounts of ceremonies and customs, which were clearly intended to be published on his return. At Tongatapu on 9 July 1777 he arrived uninvited at a ceremony, which Anderson recorded was called 'Natche' (thought to be a version of the *inasi* ceremony). Cook described it as 'an Oath of Alligiancy or solemn promise which they made the Prince as the immediate successor to' his father, Paulaho, who was the Tu'i

Tonga, the pre-eminent chief on the island.

After repeated appeals from the Tongans he agreed to 'bare my shoulders as they were' and he also let his hair down. He described how 'if I had been allowed to make use of my eyes, I might very well have seen every thing that passed, but it was necessary to sit with down cast eyes and as demure as Maids'. Baskets were carried to the high priest. 'He held each in his hand till he made a short speach or prayer, then laid it down and called for a nother and repeated the same words as before'. Following this, 'on some signal being given we all started up and ran several paces to the left and sat down with our backs to the Prince', who was presented with a piece of roasted yam. Men entered:

Engraving after John Webber, S. Middiman and J. Hall, 'The Natche, a ceremony in honour of the King's son in Tongatabo' [Tongatapu], n.d. Also published as plate 22 in Cook and King, *A voyage to the Pacific Ocean*, 1784, volume I, p. 337
British Library, Add MS 23920, f. 100

bearing large sticks or poles on their Shoulders making a noise like singing and waving their hands as they came. As soon as they got close up to us they made shew of walking very fast without advancing a single step; presently three or four men started up from the crowd with large sticks in their hands and ran to those new comers who instantly threw down the poles from their shoulders and ran off, and the others fell on these poles and beat them most unmercifully and then returned to their places.

This was followed by boxing and wrestling matches, and the ceremony ended with a speech by the chief's son.

Not all of Cook's officers approved of his participation in such ceremonies. Williamson recorded:

We who were on the outside were not a little surprised at seeing Capt Cook in ye procession of the Chiefs, with his hair hanging loose & his body naked down to ye waist, no person being admitted covered above ye waist, or with his hair tyed; I do not pretend to dispute the propriety of Capt Cook's conduct, but I cannot help thinking he rather let himself down.

Tahiti and Mo'orea

When the ships arrived at Tahiti in August 1777, preparations were being made for war over the succession to the chiefdom of the island of Mo'orea. Cook was asked to join the attack but refused: 'I was not thoroughly acquainted with the dispute and the people of Eimeo having never offended me I could take no part in it.' He described how To'ofa 'thought it strange that I who had always declared my self to be their friend would not now go and fight against their enimies'.

On 1 September a human sacrifice took place to ask Oro, the god of war, for assistance. Such sacrifices were common in times of war or misfortune. The victim was usually chosen from among enemies captured in war, people who had offended the chiefs, or from among the poorer classes. The victim would usually be ambushed and killed with blows to the back of the head before the ceremony. On learning that a victim had been killed, Cook asked to witness the ceremony. He was accompanied by Webber, Anderson and Mai. In Webber's painting Cook is shown standing at the centre of the group on the right. The man to his right may be Tu. Cook described how:

The Sacrifice was now carried to the foot of one of the small Morais before mentioned and laid down with the head towards it … The bundles of cloth were laid on the Morai and the tufts of red feathers were placed at the feet of the Sacrifice, round which the Priests placed themselves and we were now allowed to go as near as we pleased. The Chief priest made a set speach or prayer, then addressed the Sacrifice (into whom they supposed the Spirit of the Eatua was entered) in a nother, the subject of this Speach or rather prayer, was to implore the destruction of their Enim[i]es whom he mentioned several times by name.

He continued: 'From what we could learn these Sacrifices are not very uncommon, there were in the face of the Morai where this man was buried forty nine Sculls … and I have seen Sculls at many of the other great Morais'. When he explained his distaste for the custom, Mai joined in, telling To'ofa that if he had done this in England he would be hanged. Cook wrote that To'ofa exclaimed, 'vile, vile … so that we left him with as great a

opposite
John Webber,
'A Human Sacrifice
at Otaheite', 1777
British Library,
Add MS 15513, f. 16

John Webber,
'A View of Aimeo
Harbour' [Papetoai
Bay, Mo'orea], 1777
British Library,
Add MS 15513, f. 20

contempt of our customs as we could possibly have of theirs'. He also noted that To'ofa's servants 'seemed to listen with attention and were probably of a different opinion with their master'.

After leaving Tahiti the *Resolution* and *Discovery* called at Mo'orea. During their stay two goats that had been put ashore to graze were stolen. Cook wrote that 'this would have been nothing if it had not interfered with my views of Stocking other islands with these Animals'. Although one goat was returned, the other, 'a she goat and big with kid', was not. Mai and two local allies urged Cook to 'go with a party of men into the Country, and shoot every Soul I met with'. Ignoring this advice he instead marched across the island, destroying houses and canoes as he went. The destruction continued for two days, until the goat was returned.

The idyllic quality of Webber's painting contrasts with the destruction wrought by the British on the island. Cook's men were divided on the justification for his actions. King believed that:

less destructive measures might have been adoptd & the end gain'd, whether it was simply to get what was of little value or Consequence back again or in future deter them from thefts; I doubt whether our Ideas of propriety in punishing so many innocent people for the crimes of a few, will ever be reconcileable to any principle one can form of justice.

In contrast, Samwell felt that Cook's actions were justified: 'Not one of the Indians were hurt during the whole of this disagreeable Business & the whole of the Loss & Mischief fell upon the Chiefs, who brought it upon themselves, & had it in their Power to have prevented it by restoring the Goat at first.'

Although the immediate cause of Cook's actions was the theft of a goat, some historians have suggested that the severity of his response may have been prompted by his friendship with Tu and To'ofa and their enmity towards Mo'orea.

Mai returns home

This somewhat imaginative depiction of Mai's arrival in Tahiti was published in 1781 in an account of the voyage by John Rickman, the second lieutenant on the *Discovery*. It shows Mai riding a horse, wearing a suit of armour and firing a pistol. He is accompanied by Cook who is also on horseback. According to Rickman:

> *Capt. Cook, with Omai, took an airing on horseback, to the great astonishment of the inhabitants, many hundreds of whom followed them with loud acclamations. Omai, to excite their admiration the more, was dressed cap-a-pee in a suit of armour, which he carried with him, and was mounted and caparisoned with his sword and pike, like St George accoutred to kill the dragon, whom he exactly represented; only that Omai had pistols in his holsters, of which the poor saint knew not the use ... when the crowd became clamorous, and troublesome, he every now and then pulled out a pistol and fired it among them, which never failed to send them scampering away.*

In fact Mai's arrival attracted less notice than the British had expected, and he was only rarely the centre of attention. He had been given the suit of armour by Sandwich as a present and

wore it on a number of occasions. Cook recorded how Mai, dressed in the armour, was paddled around the bay in a canoe: 'every one had a full View of him but it did not draw their attention so much as might be expected'.

Cook had hoped to settle Mai at Matavai Bay under Tu's protection. However, he recorded that Mai's behaviour had alienated Tu and other senior figures, and he therefore decided to settle him on another island.

Mai's home island of Ra'iatea was still under the control of the men from Bora Bora. It was therefore decided that he should settle at Huahine, where Te Ri'itaria, the high chief, agreed to Cook's request to grant him land. This watercolour by Webber (opposite page) shows the harbour at Fare, where Mai's house was built using planks from canoes destroyed at Mo'orea. A garden was planted with vegetables and Mai was also given livestock, including horses. Cook described the transfer of consumer goods and curiosities bought in London into the house:

Amongst many other useless things, was a box of Toys which when exposed to publick view seemed to please the gazing Multitude very much; but as to his Pots, Kettles, Dishes, plates drinking mugs, glasses &c, &c, &c hardly any one so much as looked at. Omai himself now found that they were of no manner of use to him, that a baked hog eat better than a boiled one, that a plaintain leafe made as good a dish or plate as pewter and that a cocoanut shell was as good to drink out of as a black-jack.

He continued, 'I saw that he was liable to loss every thing as he had got as soon as we were gone' and therefore 'I gave out that I should return to the island again after being absent the usual time, and that if I did not find Omai in the same state as I left him all those who had been his enemy would feel the weight of my resentment'. The ship sailed on 1 November. Mai stayed on board until the last moment and 'Mr King, who went in the boat, told me that he wept all the time in going

ashore'. Te Weherua and Koa, the young Māoris who had travelled with Mai, were also left at the island.

When Bligh returned to the Society Islands in 1789 as captain of the *Bounty* he asked after Mai and wrote up the following account in his logbook:

Omai died about 30 Months after we left him, that Tiiarooah and Coah died before Omai, and all of them a natural death. That no animal remain except the Mare … The House he said was torn to pieces and Stolen [Odiddee said it was burnt down], and Omais fire Arms were at Ulieta … He told me, he and Omai often rode together, and described that Omai always rode in Boots, so that it is evident he did not immediately after our leaving him, lay aside the Englishman. Perhaps as convincing a proof as any that Omai rode often, is that several people have the representation of a Man on Horseback Tattowed on their Legs.

Cook's First Visit to Hawai'i

The ships sailed north from Huahine and on 18 January 1778 an island was sighted. This was Oahu, one of the western Hawai'ian islands. Kauai, another island in the group, was sighted soon after and a third, Niihau, the following day. The *Resolution* and *Discovery* are believed to have been the first European ships to visit Hawai'i. When some of the islanders came on board Cook wrote:

> *I never saw Indians so much astonished at the entering a ship before, their eyes were continually flying from object to object, the wildness to their looks and actions fully express'd their surprise and astonishment at the several new o[b]jects before them and envinced that they never had been on board of a ship before.*

The ships anchored in Waimea Bay, Kauai where, on 20 January, a party went ashore. Several hundred people had assembled on the beach. Cook wrote: 'the very instant I leapt ashore they all fell flat on their faces, and remained in that humble posture till I made signs to them to rise'. The following day he went inland with Anderson and Webber: 'Our guide proclaimed our approach and everyone whom we met fell on their faces and remained in that position until we passed. This, as I afterwards understood, is done to their great chiefs.' It is interesting that this was Cook's belief, given the later controversies over whether or not he was believed by the Hawai'ians to be the god Lono on his final visit to Hawai'i.

In this watercolour Webber depicts the British visit to the village of Waimea. In the foreground sailors are bartering with

John Webber, 'An Inland View
at Waimea, Atooi', 1778
British Library, Add MS 15513, f .29

local people for provisions and cloth. Barrels of water are being
rolled back to the ship and two men carry a pig strung on a
pole. One of the Hawai'ian figures, with his back to the viewer,
wears a red and yellow-feathered helmet and cloak, indicating
his high status. Cook described the scene in his journal:

> We no sooner landed, that a trade was set on foot for hogs
> and potatoes, which the people gave us in exchange for nails
> and pieces of iron formed into some things like chisels. We
> met with no obstruction in watering on the contrary the
> Natives assisted our people to roll the Casks to and from
> the pond.

The 'Polynesian Triangle'

Hawai'i forms the northern point of the 'Polynesian Triangle' and the expedition's arrival there meant that Cook had now retraced the major voyages made during the settlement of Polynesia. The language of the islanders was similar to that of the Tahitians, New Zealanders and Easter Islanders, illustrating the huge range of early migration between islands. Cook wrote of this:

How shall we account for this nation spreading itself so far over this vast ocean? We find them from New Zealand to the south, to these islands to the north, and from Easter Island to the [New] Hebrides … how much further is not known but we may safely conclude that they extend to the west beyond the [New] Hebrides.

Webber's picture (above) shows the heiau, a place of worship, that he visited with Cook and Anderson. Cook noted that this 'in many respects was like those [marae] of Otaheite'.

The Pyramid which they call [Henananoo] was erected at one end, it was 4 feet square at the base and about [20] feet high, the four sides was built of small sticks and branches, in an open manner and the inside of the pyramid was hollow or open from bottom to top. Some part of it was, or had been covered with a very thin light grey cloth, which seemed to be consecrated to Religious and ceremonious purposes, as a good deal of it was about this Morai and I had some of it forced upon me on my first landing. On each side and near the Pyrimid, stood erect some rude carved boards, exactly like those in the Morais at Otaheite.

opposite
John Webber,
[A 'heiau' at Waimea], 1778
British Library, Add MS 15513, f. 27

right
John Webber,
'An Idol made of Wicker and
covered with Red Feathers', 1778
British Library, Add MS 15514, f. 27

Venereal Disease

One of Cook's preoccupations throughout his voyages was to prevent his crew spreading sexually transmitted diseases. At Hawai'i, where his ships seemed clearly to be the first to visit from Europe, he was particularly concerned to avoid this legacy. He wrote: 'I gave orders that no women, on any account whatever were to be admitted on board the ships, I also forbade all manner of connection with them, and ordered that none who had the veneral upon them should go out of the ships'. He continued:

> It is no more than I did when I first visited the Friendly Islands yet I afterwards found it did not succeed, and I am much afraid that this will always be the case where it is necessary to have a number of people on shore; the opportunities and inducements to an intercourse between the sex, are there too many to be guarded against.

He assessed the state of medical knowledge, writing that 'it is also a doubt with me, that the most skillfull of the Faculty can tell whether every man who has had the veneral is so far cured as not to communicate it further':

> Amongst a number of men, there will be found some who will endeavour to conceal this disorder, and there are some again who care not to whom they communicate it, of this last we had an instance at Tongatabu in the Gunner of the Discovery, who remained ashore to manage the trade for Captain Clerke. After he knew he had contracted this disease he continued to sleep with different women who were supposed not to have contracted it; his companions expostulated with him without effect; till it came to the notice of Captain Clerke who ordered him on board.

On arriving at the eastern Hawai'ian islands later that year, Cook again issued orders restricting trade and preventing women from visiting the ships. However, he soon realised that the people 'were of the same Nation as those of the leeward islands, and if we did not mistake them they knew of our being there. Indeed it appeared rather too evident as these people had got amongst [them] the Veneral distemper and I as yet knew of no other way they could come by it'.

The North Pacific and the Arctic

Introduction

In sailing north to the west coast of America the expedition was sailing towards seas which were already being explored by other European nations. The Spanish claimed ownership of the west coast and, to buttress their claim, had sent an expedition led by Juan José Pérez Hernández to the North Pacific in 1774. Pérez had anchored at Nootka Sound, on what is now Vancouver Island. Further north, Russia was taking an increasing interest in the land mass opposite its eastern borders. Russian fur traders were already well established on the Aleutian Islands, which extend from Alaska towards the Russian peninsula of Kamchatka, and were beginning to explore the Alaskan coast itself.

In March 1778 the *Resolution* and *Discovery* arrived off the coast of present-day Oregon and sailed north through storms, rain and sleet, anchoring like the Spanish at Nootka Sound, where trade in furs took place. From there the ships continued north to Alaska, where the coastline was explored in a vain search for a channel to the east coast. There Cook noted that the people they met had iron and glass beads 'not of their manufacture' and initially concluded 'they may get them from some of their neighbours with whome the Russians may have a trade'. He commented that:

> *There is no doubt but a very beneficial fur trade might be carried on with the inhabitants of this vast coast, but unless a northern passage is found it seem rather too remote for Great Britain to receive any emolument from it ... a trade with foreigners would increase their wants by introducing new luxuries amongst them, in order to purchase which they would be more assiduous in procuring skins, for I think it is pretty evident they are not a scarce article in the country.*

The ships sailed west, following the Alaskan coast towards the Aleutians. On 19 June several canoes approached the *Discovery* and a man in one of them 'took of his cap and bowed after the manner of Europeans, which induced them to throw him a rope, to which he fastened a small thin wood case or box and then, after speaking something and making some more signs droped astern'. The box contained a note in Russian, a language nobody on board could read. On 28 June a party landed at Unalaska Island to take on water. A man brought on board another note in Russian. King wrote that the Russians were in 'frequent & perhaps constant intercourse with these people' who 'knew of Kamchatka, point'd to where it lay, & made us understand that they had people amongst them who came from there'.

From Unalaska the ships returned east along the northern side of the Alaskan peninsula and then followed the coast north towards the Arctic. On 3 August, the surgeon William Anderson died of tuberculosis, from which he, like Charles Clerke, had been suffering during the voyage. Cook wrote that 'he was a Sensible Young Man, an agreeable companion, well skilld in his profession, and had acquired much knowledge in other Sciences, that it pleased God to have spar'd his life might have been usefull in the Course of the Voyage'.

The ships sailed through the Bering Strait in search of the open polar sea that Daines Barrington had predicted awaited discovery there. However, they soon ran up against a barrier of sheet ice and, following this east, discovered that it extended from the west coast of North America to the east coast of Asia. In late August the expedition reached the Russian shore. Cook wrote: 'The season was now so very far advanced and the time when the frost is expected to set in so near at hand, that I did not think it consistent with prudence to make any farther

Engraving after
John Webber, 'sea otter'
British Library, Add MS 23921, f. 113

attempts to find a passage this year'. The ships sailed south through the Bering Strait.

Rather than winter in Kamchatka, Cook decided to return to Hawai'i. En route he investigated part of the Alaskan coast that had not been seen on the journey north. He had with him Staehlin's *Account of the New Northern Archipelago*, which contained a map showing Alaska as an island. King was sent north to discover 'whether the land you are then upon, suppos'd to be the Island of Alatska, is really an Isld or joins to the Land on the East supposed to be the Continent of America'. After less than a day's travel by boat he ascertained that 'our business was finish'd & that the 2 Coasts were only divided by a small river'. Cook concluded that 'Mr Staehlin's Map must be erroneous'.

The ships called at Unalaska in October on the way south, where Cook made the reluctant crew eat berries and drink spruce beer to counter the risk of scurvy. Here they made direct contact with the Russians, in the form of three fur traders, for the first time. Despite the language barrier, the Russians were able to share information on the geography of the area. They knew of Vitus Bering's 1741 expedition to Alaska but did not have 'the least idea of what part of the World *Mr Staehlins* Map refered to'. Cook showed them his own chart and found that 'they were strangers to every part of the America Coast except what lies opposite to them'.

Soon after, Gerassim Gregoriev Ismailov, 'the principal person amongst the Russians in this and the neighbouring islands', arrived. Cook described him as 'very well acquainted

with the Geography of these parts and with all the discoveries the Russians had made and [he] at once pointed out the errors of the Modern Maps'. He confirmed that 'the Russians have made several attempts to get a footing upon that part of the Continent which lies adjacent to the islands but have allways been repulsed by the Natives'. Ismailov allowed Cook to copy his charts. Cook wrote of him that he:

seemed to have abilities to intitle him to a higher station in life than that in which he was employed, he was tolerably well versed in Astronomy and other necessary parts of the Mathematicks. I complemented him with an Hadley's Octant and altho it was the first he had perhaps ever seen, yet he made himself acquainted with most of the uses that instrument is capable of in a very short time.

During their stay visits were made to the nearby Russian settlement and more was discovered about the extent of the Russian presence in the Aleutians. Cook wrote:

There are Russians on all the principal Islands between this and Kamtschatka, for the sole purpose of furing, and the first and great object is the Sea Beaver or Otter ... I never thought to ask how long it was since they got a footing on Oonalaska and the neighbouring isles, but to judge from the great subjection the Natives are under, it must have been some time.

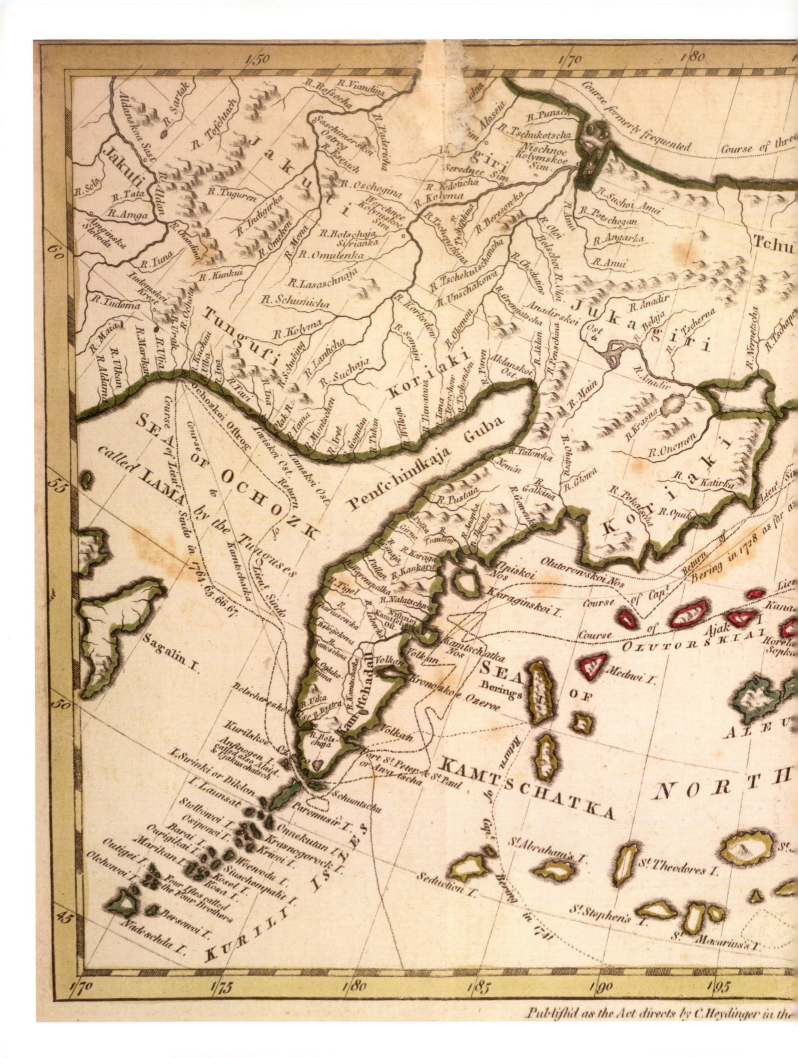

Map labels (as transcribed):

Top margin coordinates: 150 · 170 · 180

Left margin coordinates: 60 · 55 · 50 · 45

Bottom margin coordinates: 170 · 175 · 180 · 185 · 190 · 195

Course formerly frequented · Course of three

JAKUTI

R. Viandina · R. Rofsocha · R. Zadernicha · Alaseia · R. Punsch · R. Tschukotscha · Nischnoe Kolymskoe Sim.

R. Sartak · R. Tofchtach · Saschimerskoi Ostrog · R. Ischiach · R. Oschogina · gir
Aldanskoa Soot · R. Sola · R. Tata · R. Amga · R. Aldan · R. Tuguren · R. Indigirka · R. Onelboti · R. Mona · R. Omelenka · R. Kedotucha · R. Kolyma · Serednee Sim.

Tchu

R. Luna · R. Kunkui · R. Schumicha · R. Omelenka · R. Lasaschnaja · R. Schumicha · R. Kolyma · R. Lanhcha · R. Suchaja · R. Tschekutschancha · R. Stachoi Ama · R. Potschogan · R. Angarka · R. Anui

Tungusi · Koriaki · Jukagiri · Juka giri

Anadirskoi Ost · R. Anadir · Belaja · R. Tscherna

Koriaki · Koriaki

Penfchinskaja Guba

SEA OF OCHOZK called LAMA by the Tungouses

Sagalin I.

Bering in 1728 as far as

Olutoron'skoi Nos · Tpiskoi Nos · Karaginskoi I.

Course of Capt. · OLUTORSKIAI

Kamtschatka Nos · Mednoi I. · SEA OF · Bering's

Otschadall · Volkan · Hronozlzkoe Ozere · ALEU

KAMTSCHATKA · NORTH

Kurilskoe Ozero · Anstpogen I. called also Alait & Gakus chasoch
I. Swinki or Diklon · I. Launsat · Paromusir I. · KURILI IS.

St. Abraham's I. · St. Theodores I.
Stolbovoi I. · Onnekutan I. · Krasnogorovck I.
Osipovoi I. · Kriwoi I.
Barai I. · Woenoda I.
Ouriplkai I. · Siuschenpalit I.
Marikan I. · Kosel I.
Outigoi I. · Kosa I.
Olchovoi I. · Four Ifles called the Four Brothers
Persovoi I.
Nadeschda I. · KURILI IS. · Seduction I. · St. Stephen's I. · St. Macarius's I.

Publifh'd as the Act directs by C. Heydinger in the

Staehlin's map supposedly showed new discoveries by Russian traders, and depicted Alaska as an island. It is so inaccurate that some scholars have suggested it was deliberately designed to confuse other European powers.

Jacob von Staehlin,
A map of the new northern archipelago discovered by the Russians in the Seas of Kamtschatka & Anadir, published in *An Account of the New Northern Archipelago*, 1774
British Library, 979.h.2.

John Webber,
'A View in Ship Cove', 1778
British Library, Add MS 15514, f. 10

Trade in Nootka Sound

This drawing shows the *Resolution* at anchor in Nootka Sound in late March or April 1778, surrounded by canoes. The area was inhabited by the Mowachaht, part of the Nuu-chah-nulth nation. In one canoe a man stands upright wearing a large headdress, with his hand outstretched. Cook described how, on their first arrival, the people in the canoes would perform 'a singular ceremony':

> *They would paddle with all thier strength quite round both Ships, A Chief or other principal person standing up with a Spear, or some other Weapon in his hand and speaking, or rather holloaing all the time, sometimes this person would have his face cover[ed] with a mask, either that of the human face or some animal, and some times instead of a weapon hold in his hand a rattle. After making the circuit of the ships they would come along side and begin to trade without further ceremony.*

Webber's depiction emphasises the role of trade in establishing peaceful relations between ship and shore. Cook, who had been instructed to seek trading opportunities by the Admiralty, described the goods exchanged:

> *Their articles were the Skins of various animals, such as Bears, Wolfs, Foxes, Dear, Rackoons, Polecats, Martins and in particular the Sea Beaver, the same as is found on the coast of Kamchatka … they took in exchange, Knives, chissels, pieces of iron & Tin, Nails, Buttons, or any kind of metal. Beads they were not fond of and cloth of all kinds they rejected.*

Before the ships departed on 26 April Cook exchanged a beaver-skin cloak for a new broadsword with the local Mowachaht chief, 'which made him happy as a prince. He as also many others importuned us much to return to them and by way of incouragement promised to lay in a good stock of skins for us, and I have not the least doubt but they will'.

Houses at Nootka Sound

This picture is believed to show the village of Yuquot (the name of the village means 'where the winds blow from many directions'). The British visited the village in April 1778. King noted 'upon one building in the West town was a tree supported by two posts of an uncommon size, capable of making a Mast for a first rate. It must have requir'd no small force to have placed it, Although they cou'd perceive no use or end that it could Answer'. King's description is consistent with the building on the right of the picture. Cook described the buildings:

Some of which are one hundred and fifty feet in length, twenty four or thirty broad and seven or eight feet high from the floor to the roof, which in them all is flat and covered with loose boards. The Walls, or sides and ends, are also built up of boards and the framing consi[s]ts of large trees or logs.

At Nootka Sound the task of collecting fodder for the animals on board led to complex negotiations. Cook wrote of:

About a dozen men who all laid cla[i]m to some part of the grass which I purchased of them and as I thought liberty to cut where ever I pleased, but here again I was misstaken, for the liberal manner I had paid the first pretended pr[oprietors brought more upon me and there was not a blade of grass that had not a seperated owner, so that I very soon emptied my pockets with purchasing.

John Webber,
'A View of Snug Corner Cove',
1778
British Library, Add MS 15514, f. 8

Prince William Sound, Alaska

The ships left Nootka Sound at the end of April 1778 and followed the coast north towards Alaska. The *Resolution* had sprung a leak during the voyage north and in May the ships anchored in a bay that was later called Prince William Sound to make repairs. The need to find safe harbour is perhaps reflected in Cook's naming of the anchorage 'Snug Corner Bay', despite the harshness of the weather. Webber's drawing shows the ships at anchor, with the towering peaks of the Chugach Mountains in the background.

Samwell recorded that the local people 'sold us Furs & other things for iron & beads, they were exceedingly fond of blue & green beads many of which they had among them before we came here'. He continued:

> How they got them was the Subject about which many Conjectures were formed, it did not seem probable that they had got them from the Southward along the Coast, for we did not see a Single bead among the Indians of George's Sound, it afforded a plausibility of a Passage by which they might have come from the other side of the Continent; however this corresponded more with our wishes than our Hopes, as there was still another way for them to come & that the most likely, which was from the Russians of Kamtschatka who we had reason to suppose traded with the Indians along the American Coast for their Furs.

John Webber,
[Portrait of a Woman of Prince
William Sound], 1778
British Library, Add MS 15514, f. 11

A Woman of Prince William Sound

Cook rarely noted the names of the people he met in the North
Pacific. However, as during the earlier part of the voyage, his
interest in ethnographic detail led him to record long accounts
of culture and society. At Prince William Sound he wrote:

*These people are not of the same Nation as those who Inhabit
King Georges Sound [Nootka Sound], both their language
and features are wid[e]ly different: These are small of stature,
but thick set good looking people and from Crantz description
of the Greenlander, seem to bear some affinity to them. But as
I never saw a Greenlander or an Esquemaus, who are said to
be of the same nation, I cannot be a sufficient judge and as we
may very probably see more of them I shall reserve the
discussion of this point to some other time.*

Webber's portrait shows a woman from Prince William
Sound. In his journal Cook wrote a detailed description of the
appearance, clothing and jewellery of the women of the area:

*I saw not a woman with a head dress of any kind, they had
all long black hair a part of which was tied up in a bunch
over the forehead … Though the lips of all were not slit, yet
all were bored, especially the women and even the young
girls; to these holes and slits they fix pieces of bone of this size
and shape, placed side by side in the inside of the lip; a
thread is run through them to keep them together, and some
goes quite through the lip and fastens, or fore-locks on the
out side to which they hang other pieces of bone or beads.
This Ornament is a very great impediment to the speach and
makes them look as if they had a double row of teeth in the
under jaw. Besides these lip-jewels which they seemed to
value above all others, they wear a bone, or some bugle
beads strung on a stif string or Cord 3 or 4 inch long, run
through the cartilage that divides the nostrils from each
other. Their ears are bored all round to which they hang
beads or pieces of bone.*

Alaska and the Aleutian Islands

After leaving Prince William Sound, the ships continued north, spending several days investigating a broad inlet, which Gore believed was the entry to the Northwest Passage. After sailing about a hundred miles (160 kilometres) up the inlet, the ships anchored near the site of what would later become the city of Anchorage. During the journey Samwell recorded that the ships were visited by people in canoes every day, 'who sold us fine Sea Beaver & other Skins for Iron, and they also sold us some excellent Salmon & Hallybut fresh & dried, curious Quivers for Nails & other trifles'.

By now it was becoming clearer that Alaska was part of the mainland and not an island. Cook wrote:

We were now convinced that the Continent extended farther to the west than from Modern Charts we had reason to expect and made a passage into Baffin or Hudson bays far less probable, or at least made it of a greater extent. But if I had not examined this place it would have been concluded, nay asserted that it communicated with the sea to the north, or with one of these bays to the east.

King was sent ashore to display the flag and take possession of the country and river. On shore he met a party of about a dozen people, who were 'very Civil in their manner, yet suspicious'. Anderson exchanged a pair of buckles for a dog, which promptly bit him and was shot on the beach. At this the people retreated and 'not one would come near us'.

The expedition continued to the Aleutian Islands, where a stop was made at Unalaska in June 1778. On a trip ashore Webber made this drawing of a woman and Samwell later wrote up an account in his journal:

We met with a very beautiful young Woman accompanied by her Husband who having some Ornaments about her we had not noticed before, & being altogether very prettily dressed Mr. Webber was willing to have a sketch of her, and as we had time enough on our Hands we sat down together and he made a drawing of her; we were all charmed with the good nature and affability with which she complyed with our Wishes in staying to have her picture drawn, & with what readiness she stood up or sat down according as she was desired, seeming very much pleased in having an opportunity to oblige us.

Meanwhile, King investigated the nature of the Russian presence in the islands. He wrote that the islanders 'universally were fond of Snuff, & all chew'd tobacco, which they told us came from Kamchatka. We saw the Policy of the Russians in introducing such aquir'd tastes':

By its becoming a necessary part of their subsistence; & the effects were visible, for the Natives were not only without Skins to barter, but it appeared evident that they could not afford any for their own cloathing, which was almost entirely made of the Skins of Birds, their women only wearing Seal skin dresses, in these dresses they would have small Strips by way of Ornament of the Sea Otter.

John Webber,
[Two Chukchi People of
Chukotskiy peninsula], 1778
British Library, Add MS 15514, f. 16

The Chukotskiy Peninsula

The ships continued north to the Bering Strait and, on 9 August 1778, sighted a headland that Cook called Cape Prince of Wales, which was 'the more remarkable by being the Western extremity of all America hitherto known'. From there, the ships sailed west to the northern coast of Asia. A party landed at a village where, in Cook's words, they:

Found 40 or 50 men each armed with a spontoon bow and arrows drawn up on a rising ground on which the village stood. … As we drew near three of them came down towards the shore and were so polite as to take off their caps and make us a low bow; we returned the compliment but this did not inspire them with sufficient confidence to wait our landing, for the Moment we put the boats ashore they retired. I followed them alone without any thing in my hand, and by signs and actions got them to stop and receive some trifles I presented them with and in return they gave me two fox skins and a couple of Sea horse [walrus] teeth … they seemed very fearfull and causious … in proportion as I advanced they retreated backwards always in the attitude of being ready to make use of their Spears.

The Chuchki people lived in the Chukotskiy peninsula in northwest Siberia. The area had been incorporated into the Russian Empire during the previous decades and had seen brutal conflict between the Russians and local tribes. During the stay Webber made this drawing and Cook described the people:

The Spears or Spontoons were of Iron or steel and of European or Asiatic workmanship … the arrows they carried in a leather quiver … some of the quivers were extremely beautifull, being made of red leather on which was very neat embroidery and other ornaments … Thier cloathing consisted of a Cap, a Frock, a pair of Breeches, and a pair of boots, all made of leather.

The Arctic

The ships crossed the Arctic Circle and reached 70° 41' north on 18 August 1778. Cook wrote: 'Some time before noon we perceived a brigh[t]ness in the Northern horizon like that reflected from ice, commonly called the blink … at 1pm the sight of a large field of ice left us in no longer doubt … the ice was quite impenetrable and extend[ed] from WBS to EBN as far as the eye could reach'. The following day he reported: 'We were at this time in 20 fathoms Water, close to the edge of the ice which was as compact as a Wall and seemed to be ten or twelve feet high at least, but farther North it appeared much higher … we now stood to the Southward'. The edge of the American continent was sighted and Cook named it Icy Cape. Samwell recorded that 'we joined the Ice very near all across from the Coast of America to that of Asia'.

The ships turned south to avoid being trapped between ice and shore but on 19 August returned north, where they soon encountered the ice sheet: 'On the ice lay a prodigious number of Sea horses [Walruses] and as we were in want of fresh provisions the boats from each ship were sent to get some.' This engraving is based on an original drawing by Webber. Ignoring the objections of many of his men to the taste of the meat, Cook noted that 'we lived upon them so long as they lasted and there were few on board who did not prefer it to salt meat'. The oil burned well and the skins were used to repair rigging. After killing a large number of walruses, Cook wrote: 'They did not appear to us to be that dangerous animal some Authors have discribed'.

Engraving after
John Webber, 'Sea Horses'
British Library, Add MS 23921, f. 112

A Family at Norton Sound

The ships returned south, anchoring at Norton Sound on the coast of Alaska, where several days were spent exploring in search of a passage inland. The British met with a number of people during their stay, and these encounters were peaceful and mostly unremarkable. Samwell wrote:

> This part of the Coast is but thinly inhabited, the Houses are built together in small Villages on the Sea Shore but we saw a lonely hut here & there on the flat Land at a great distance from any others ... They are built of different Shapes but mostly square, they are but small, will not contain above 6 or 7 people conveniently; some of them have flat roofs others slanting, they are abt six feet high in the middle & 5 or six yards long & as many broad; the sides of some of them are made by laying one Timber on another horizontally, others are constructed with Timbers fixed in the Ground & slanting obliquely upwards, with the interstices filed up with Grass; the Tops are covered with Grass & stones.

Webber's watercolour may be based on a meeting with a family that took place on 13 September 1778. King described how 'the good Woman had a Child upon her back, cover'd with the hood of her Jacket; I thought it some bundle till it began to whimper, but on the womans saying some words in a Soothing tone, it remain'd very quiet'. Cook traded four knives for 400 pounds of fish and gave some beads to the little girl 'on which the Mother fell a crying, then the Father, then the other man and at last to compleat the consort the child but this Musick continued not long'.

John Webber,
[Inhabitants of Norton Sound
and their Habitations], 1778
British Library, Add MS 15514, f. 18

The Second Visit to Hawai'i

The ships sailed south for the winter and on 26 November 1778 sighted Maui, one of the eastern Hawai'ian islands. Cook wrote: 'We saw people on several parts of the coast, some houses and plantations, and the Country seemed to be both well wooded and Watered, the latter was seen falling into the Sea in several places'. On 30 November Kalani'opu'u, the high chief of Hawai'i, who the British called Teereeoboo, came on board the ship. Cook wrote that 'he made me a present of two or three small pigs and we got by barter from the other people a little fruit … in the evening we discovered another island to the windward which the natives call O'wy'he'.

The ships spent several weeks circling the island of Hawai'i without landing, partly owing to bad weather and the lack of a suitable harbour but also because Cook wanted to control trade with the Hawai'ians. During this period canoes came off from shore regularly to trade provisions. Bligh was sent ashore to assess the coast but 'found no fresh water … and that the surface of the Country was wholy composed of large slags and ashes here and there partly covered with plants'.

The last entry in Cook's journal was written on 6 January 1779, but he continued to write short entries in a log book for a further ten days. On 16 January the ships arrived off Kealakekua Bay on the west coast of Hawai'i. Cook described how 'Canoes now began to come off from all parts, so that before 10 oclock there were not less than a thousand about the two Ships … Not a man had with him a Weapon of any sort, Trade and curiosity alone brought them off'. However, thefts took place and he ordered warning shots fired from muskets and cannons. He wrote:

I have no where in this Sea seen such a number of people assembled at one place, besides those in the Canoes all the Shore of the bay was covered with people and hundreds were swiming about the Ships like shoals of fish. We should have found it difficult to have kept them in order had not a Chief or Servant of Terrioboos named Parea now and then [exerted] his authority by turning or rather driving them all out of the Ships.

John Webber,
'A View of Kealakekua Bay', 1779
British Library, Add MS 17277, f. 30

Bligh reported there was a good anchorage and fresh water and Cook decided to refit the ships in the bay. On 17 January Cook wrote: 'In the after noon I went a shore to view the place, accompanied by Touahah [a priest], Parea, Mr King and others; as soon as we landed Touahah took me by the hand and conducted me to a large Morai, the other gentlemen with Parea and four or five more of the Natives followed'. These are the last words in his logbook and after this his actions are known only from the journals of others on the expedition.

The ships had arrived at the beginning of the religious festival of Makahiki, during which Lono, the god of peace and prosperity, was in ascendency over Ku, who was represented on Earth by Kalaniʻopuʻu. Although some historians have argued that Cook was believed to be an incarnation of Lono, others have argued that he was simply seen as a very powerful chief, and therefore treated with great reverence. King's journal provides an account of the landing at Kealakekua Bay. He described how, as Cook was led to the *heiau*, or temple, of Hikau, the Hawaiʻians prostrated themselves before him. During a long ceremony

Cook, following the example of Koah, one of the priests, prostrated himself before the image of the war god Ku. King recorded that Cook was referred to by the priests as 'Erono'.

After the ceremony, a site was chosen to establish a camp and King described how it was to be 'tabooed, & that we would pay a recompense to the Owner of the ground; all of which was very readily Assented to'. Kalaniʻopuʻu arrived on 26 January 1779, after which the taboo was lifted, and cordial relations were cemented with trade and displays of boxing and wrestling. Kalaniʻopuʻu presented Cook with his own cloak and feathered cap, as well as a further five or six cloaks, four large hogs and other provisions. Cook and Kalaniʻopuʻu exchanged names and 'ratified a firm friendship'. Kalaniʻopuʻu's sons were in attendance and the eldest, a sixteen-year-old boy, slept on the *Resolution* that night.

By the end of January, with repairs to the ships completed, Cook began to think about leaving the islands. On 1 February he asked King to find out whether the Hawaiʻians would sell 'some of the pales' that ran round the *heiau*. This was agreed but

King discovered that as well as the pales, 'The Sailors were also moving off their Carved Images, & before I was aware of it had got down to the boats all the Semicircle'. Realising that this had caused offence, King consulted Koah who 'desir'd only that we would return the little Image, & to leave standing the two in the Center of the Morai'.

The ships sailed out of the bay on 4 February, guided by Koah who King later noted 'changed his name for Britanee'. On reflecting on their stay at Hawai'i, King wrote:

It is very clear from these, as well as from many other Circumstances, that they regard us as a Set of beings infinitely their superiors; should this respect wear away from familiarity, or by length of intercourse, their behaviour may change; but the common people which are generally the most troublesome, are I am afraid here kept in so slavish a subordination to their Chiefs, that I doubt whether they would venture to give us offence without great encouragement in doing so from their Masters.

Soon after their departure a storm blew up and the *Resolution*'s foremast was damaged, forcing the ships to return to the bay.

The British soon discovered that they had arrived at a time when it was taboo for canoes to enter or leave the bay, as Kalani'opu'u was away. He returned on 13 February. Burney wrote that he 'was very inquisitive, as were several of the Owhyhe Chiefs, to know the reason of our return and appeared much dissatisfied with it'.

Over the following days tensions began to rise. When a man was caught stealing the armourer's tongs, Cook ordered that he be given forty lashes, an extreme sentence at the time. On shore the watering party reported that 'the Indians had now arm'd themselves with Stones, & were still more insolent'. King sought help from 'some of the Chiefs present [and] the mob was driven away'. Further incidents took place, including the armourer's tongs again being taken and a party of sailors in boats being attacked by men throwing stones. Soon after, Cook is reported to have given orders that 'on the first appearance of throwing stones or behaving insolently, to fire ball at the offenders'.

Overnight on 14 February 1779 the large cutter from the *Discovery* disappeared. As he had done in other places, Cook went on shore with the marines to take a senior figure hostage in order to demand the return of the boat. Clerke later recorded that, on finding Kalani'opu'u having just woken up, Cook believed him to be 'quite innocent of what happen'd and

proposed to the old Gentleman to go onboard with him, which he readily agree'd to'. As the party returned to the beach, where two or three thousand people had assembled, tensions increased. News may have reached the crowd of the death of a man shot by British sailors who were blockading the harbour. Kalani'opu'u's wife and two chiefs advised him not to go on board, at which he 'appear'd dejected and frighten'd'. Cook is reported to have said, 'we can never think of compelling him to go onboard without killing a number of these People'.

The surviving accounts of Cook's death are confused and, in places, contradictory. Molesworth Phillips, the lieutenant of marines, who was on shore at the time, believed Cook was about to give orders to embark when he was confronted by:

A fellow arm'd with a long Iron Spike (which they call a Pah'hoo'ah) and a Stone; this Man made a flourish with his Pah'hoo'ah, and threatened to throw his stone upon which Capt Cook discharg'd a load of small shot at him but he having his Mat on the small shot did not penetrate it and had no other effect than further to provoke and encourage them.

Cook fired the other barrel, loaded with ball, and killed a man before the Hawai'ians 'made a general attack'. Phillips recorded that 'the Capt gave orders to the Marines to fire and afterward called out "Take to the Boats"'. Cook was killed on the beach alongside four of the marines. Sixteen Hawai'ians are believed to have been killed.

opposite
An engraving after John Webber. It shows Cook seated between three of his officers during a welcoming ceremony at Hawai'i. King described how a priest brought a pig, which 'was held up, sometimes under the Captains nose, & at last laid with a Coco nut at his feet; afterwards the Performers sat down, Kava was made & presented, a fat hog cut up & we were fed as before'.
British Library, Add MS 23921, f.75

above
This engraving from the account of the voyage by John Rickman (*Journal of Captain Cook's Last Voyage to the Pacific Ocean on Discovery*, 1781) was the first image of Cook's death to be published.
British Library, 978.l.26

himself shot the Indian the Water. Captain Cook was now the only Man on the Rock, he was seen walking down towards the Pinnace, holding his left hand against the Back of his head to guard it from the Stones & carrying his musket under the other Arm. An Indian came running behind him, stopping once or twice as he advanced, as if he was afraid that he should turn round, then taking him unaware he sprung to him knocked him on the back of his head with a large Club taken out of a fence & instantly fled with the greatest precipitation, the blow made Captain Cook stagger two or three paces, he then fell on his hand & one knee & dropped his musket, as he was rising another Indian came running to him & before he could recover himself from the Fall

David Samwell's Account

This is David Samwell's manuscript description of the death of James Cook, a version of which was later published. Samwell describes how, after the violence began, Cook 'was seen walking down towards the Pinnace, holding his left hand against the back of his head to guard it from the stones' and relates his being hit 'with a large club' before being stabbed in the back of the neck with an iron dagger. Samwell then records Cook struggling in the water and waving for help to the men in the pinnace, just offshore, 'which it seems it was not in their Power to give'. After this, Cook 'endeavoured to scramble on the Rock when a fellow gave him a blow on the head with a large Club and he was seen alive no more.'

David Samwell journal
British Library, Egerton 2591, f. 201

drew out an iron Dagger he concealed under his
feathered Cloak & Struck it with all his force
into the back of his Neck, which made Capt Cook
tumble into the water in a kind of a bite
by the side of the Rock where the water is about
knee deep, here he was followed by a croud of people
who endeavoured to keep him under water but
struggling very strong with them he got his
head up & looking towards the Pinnace which
was not above a boat hook's Length from him
waved his hands to them for assistance which
it seems it was not in their Power to give
the Indians got him under water again but he
disengaged himself & got his head up once
more & not being able to swim he endeavoured
to scramble on the Rock when a fellow gave
him a blow on the head with a large Club
and he was seen alive no more, they now kept
him under water, one man sat on his Shoulders
& beat his head with a Stone while others beat
him with Clubs & Stones, they then hauled him
up dead on the Rocks where they stuck him
with their Daggers, dashed his head against
the rock & beat him with Clubs & Stones

left
Engraving by Francesco
Bartolozzi and William Byrne,
after John Webber,
The Death of Captain Cook
British Library, Add MS 23921, f. 69

overleaf
John Cleveley Jr.,
The Death of Cook, c. 1780
Private collection

Contrasting Depictions of James Cook's Death

After his return to Britain, John Webber created two paintings depicting Cook's death. These show him apparently calling to his men to cease firing, while behind him a man with a dagger is poised to stab him. Webber's paintings were the basis of this print (left), which was widely sold in Britain in the 1780s and did much to promote the image of Cook as peacemaker. Some versions of it appeared with the caption *The Death of Captain Cook… by the Murdering Dagger of a Barbarian at Carakooa… He having there become a Victim to his own Humanity.*

The painting overleaf is by John Cleveley, whose brother James sailed on Cook's third voyage. It is believed to date from around 1780 and shows a notably aggressive Cook leading his men in an attack. His gun is empty and he is using it as a club, swinging it with anger and force. By contrast, in a later painting Cleveley, perhaps influenced by Webber's depiction, showed Cook as a peacemaker, seeking to prevent further bloodshed.

After Cook's Death: Completing the Voyage

Charles Clerke, who was now in charge of the expedition, sent boats to the shore under a white flag to request Cook's body. On 16 February a priest named Car'na'care, who was known to King, came on board with a 'large piece of Flesh' that was believed to have been a part of Cook's thigh. Clerke wrote:

The poor fellow told us that all of the rest of the Flesh had been burnt at different places with some peculiar kind of ceremony, that this had been deliver'd to him for that purpose, but as we appear'd anxious to recover the Body he had brought us all that he could get of it, he likewise added that the Bones which were all that now remain'd were in the possession of King Terre'oboo.

Although a popular myth exists that Cook's body was eaten, in fact the flesh was removed from the bodies of deceased chiefs in order to distribute the bones as powerful relics.

The following day the sailors landed on shore and burned a village, killing many people. Clerke ordered that the guns be fired from the ship, bringing further destruction. In the evening two Hawai'ian leaders came on board and 'beg'd we would fire at them no more'. On 20 February Cook's remains were returned and were

This watercolour by John Webber shows the village of Paratounqua (Paratunka). David Samwell described it as 'about 20 miles from the harbour of St Peter and Paul, [it] contains a Church, six Russian Houses and 16 Balagans or Kamtschadale Houses built upon high Pillars and a few Joortas or Huts built partly underground'.
British Library, Add MS 15514, f. 30

committed to the sea the next day. The ships sailed from the bay on 23 February 1779. Clerke completed the charting of the islands and took on further supplies before sailing north again in search of the Northwest Passage. At the end of April, the ships anchored at the village of Petropavlovsk on the Kamchatka peninsula, where the Russian governor provided supplies free of charge, apparently in recognition of Cook's role in improving diplomatic relations with the Chuchki people.

On 6 July 1779 the ships passed through the Bering Strait again but were soon blocked by ice. Later that month two polar bears were shot and the meat found to be more edible than the walrus meat Cook had made his men eat the previous year. Clerke took the ships south again to Kamchatka, where he died in late August of the tuberculosis he had contracted in prison. John Gore now became leader of the expedition, the ships returning to Britain via China and the Cape of Good Hope. At Macao, the East India Company's trading post in China, sea otter pelts were sold for substantial profits. News of this would lead to a flood of British trading expeditions to the Pacific Northwest over the following decade.

CONCLUSION

It was not until June 1784 that the official account of the voyage was published. It was authored by James King, who had sailed with Cook, and Canon John Douglas, who had helped him prepare the account of the second voyage. An expensive three-volume work, it included plates based on Webber's drawings and maps showing Cook's charting of the Pacific. The passage describing Cook's death included the following:

Our unfortunate Commander, the last time he was seen distinctly, was standing at the water's edge, and calling out to the boats to cease firing, and to pull in. If it be true, as some of those present have imagined, that the marines and boatmen had fired without his orders, and that he was desirous of preventing any further bloodshed, it is not improbable that his humanity, on this occasion, proved fatal to him.

The script and stage set for the 1785 pantomime *Omai, or a Trip Round the World* took the commemoration of Cook to a new level. Webber acted as an advisor and contributed to the painting of the scenery and the design of the costumes. The pantomime, which includes a cast of characters assembled from Cook's three voyages, depicts Mai as the son of Tu. He is watched over by To'ofa ('Protector of the legal Kings of Otaheite') and challenged by Hitihiti ('Oediddee, Pretender to the Throne'), who is supported by Oberea ('an Enchantress'). Other characters include Britannia (played by 'Mrs Inchbald') and Londinia ('the consort destined to Omia').

The play culminates with a procession at Tahiti of 'the Deputies from the different quarters of the globe that have been visited by Capt. Cook &c bearing presents and congratulations to Omai, on his advancement to the throne of his Ancestors'. The procession is led by a Tahitian dancing girl and includes groups from New Zealand, Tanna, Tonga, Hawai'i, Easter Island, Russia,

Kamchatka, the Chukchi Peninsula, Nootka Sound and Unalaska. During the procession news arrives of the death of Cook at Hawai'i. The play ends with a song eulogising him:

He came, and he saw, not to conquer but to save;
The Caesar of Britain was he;
Who scorn'd the ambition of making a slave
While Britons themselves are so free.
Now the Genius of Britain forbids us to grieve,
Since Cook, ever Honour'd, immortal shall live.

During the song a painted backdrop entitled *The Apotheosis of Captain Cook* was lowered. It showed Cook being borne up to heaven while below him the battle rages in Kealakekua Bay. It was later published as an engraving by the play's producer, Philippe de Loutherbourg.

There matters might have rested, but for events taking place elsewhere in London. In summer 1785 the House of Commons held an inquiry into the problem of prison overcrowding. In the decades before the American War of Independence approximately 50,000 convicts had been transported to the American colonies. Since the outbreak of war this option had been closed off and large numbers of convicts were being held in overcrowded gaols and prison ships. In 1779 Joseph Banks had first recommended to the Commons that Botany Bay, 'which was about seven months voyage from England', would make an ideal site for a prison colony:

There would be little probability of any Opposition from the natives, as, during his stay there, in the year 1770, he saw very few, and did not think there were above fifty in all the neighbourhood … the climate, he apprehended, was similar to that about Toulouse in the South of France … the proportion of rich soil was small in comparison to the

The APOTHEOSIS of CAPTAIN COOK.

From a Design of P. J. De Loutherbourg, R.A. *The View of* KARAKAKOOA BAY *Is from a Drawing by* John Webber, R.A *(the last he made) in the Collection of* Mr G. Baker.

barren, but sufficient to support a very large number of people ... he did not doubt but our oxen and sheep, if carried there would thrive and increase ... the grass was long and luxuriant, and there were some eatable vegetables, particularly a sort of wild spinage; the country was well supplied with water; there was an abundance of timber and fuel.

Banks's solution was not adopted at the time, not least because it still seemed possible that British victory would lead to the resumption of transportation to North America. After American independence pressure for a solution increased and Australia was one of a number of locations considered. In August 1786 Lord Sydney, the home secretary, announced the government's decision to establish a prison colony at Botany Bay in New South Wales. Historians still debate the extent to which the decision to establish the colony was simply designed to rid Britain of its convicts and the extent to which longer-term strategic considerations of trade and empire underlay it.

The nineteenth century saw more systematic European intervention in the Pacific. By the end of the century Britain had colonised Australia, New Zealand and the west coast of Canada. France had annexed the Society Islands, including Tahiti, and New Caledonia. Alaska had been incorporated into the Russian Empire and later sold to the USA. The USA had also taken control of the Hawai'ian Islands. Alongside territorial expansion came a range of other European interventions, including traders seeking profits from the natural environment, missionaries seeking to bring the Christian religion to the Pacific, planters seeking to acquire land, and increasing numbers of migrants seeking a new life.

The extent to which this later history was a legacy of Cook's voyages is a subject that is both complex and deeply contested. At its simplest, Cook's determination to fulfil his Admiralty instructions (in Johann Forster's despairing words 'to leave nothing to chance & future explorers') means that his voyages stand out for the extent to which they were successful in charting the remaining blank spaces on European maps of the Pacific. Since Cook's charts guided later European visitors to the Pacific, whether traders, colonisers, missionaries, planters or migrants, his voyages will probably always be viewed as a symbolic starting point for the changes these visitors brought.

John Webber
[View of Macao]
British Library, Add MS 15514, f. 41.

Further Reading

Published Accounts and Edited Journals

John Beaglehole (ed.),
The Endeavour Journal of Sir Joseph Banks, 1768–1771 (Sydney, 1962)

John Beaglehole (ed.),
The Journals of Captain James Cook on his Voyages of Discovery
(Cambridge, 1955–74)

James Cook,
A Voyage Towards the South Pole and Round the World
(London, 1777)

James Cook and James King,
A Voyage to the Pacific Ocean, undertaken by Command of His Majesty for Making Discoveries in the Northern Hemisphere
(London, 1784)

Philip Edwards (ed.),
James Cook: The Journals
(London, 1999)

Georg Forster,
A Voyage Round the World in His Britannic Majesty's Sloop, Resolution
(London, 1777)

John Hawkesworth,
An Account of the Voyages undertaken … for Making Discoveries in the Southern Hemisphere
(London, 1773)

Michael Hoare (ed.),
The Resolution Journal of Johann Reinhold Forster 1772–1775
(London, 1982)

Stanfield Parkinson,
A Journal of a Voyage to the South Seas, in His Majesty's Ship, The Endeavour. Faithfully Transcribed from the Papers of the Late Sydney Parkinson
(London, 1773)

Secondary Sources

Atholl Anderson, Judith Binney and Aroha Harris,
Tangata Whenua: An Illustrated History
(Wellington, 2014)

James Barnett and David Nicandri,
Arctic Ambitions: Captain Cook and the Northwest Passage
(Seattle and London, 2015)

John Beaglehole,
The Life of Captain James Cook
(London, 1974)

Harold Carter, 'Notes on the Drawings by an Unknown Artist from the Voyage of HMS *Endeavour*' in Margarette Lincoln (ed.), *Science and Exploration in the Pacific*
(Woodbridge, 1998), pp. 133–34

Harold Carter,
Sir Joseph Banks, 1743–1820
(London, 1988)

Andrew David, Rüdiger Joppien and Bernard Smith,
The Charts and Coastal Views of Captain Cook's Voyages
(London, 1988–97)

Anne Di Piazza and Erik Pearthree,
'A New Reading of Tupaia's Chart' in *The Journal of the Polynesian Society*,
Vol. 116, No. 3 (Sept. 2007), pp. 321–40

Joan Druett,
Tupaia: Captain Cook's Polynesian Navigator
(Santa Barbara, 2011)

Lars Eckstein and Anja Schwarz,
'The Making of Tupaia's Map'
(in preparation)

John Gascoigne,
Joseph Banks and the English Enlightenment: Useful Knowledge and Polite Culture
(Cambridge, 1994)

Richard Holmes,
The Age of Wonder
(London, 2008)

Tony Horwitz,
Into the Blue: Boldly Going Where Captain Cook Has Gone Before
(Crows Nest, NSW, 2002)

Richard Hough,
Captain James Cook
(London, 1994)

Rüdiger Joppien and Bernard Smith,
The Art of Captain Cook's Voyages
(New Haven and London, 1985–87)

Peter Marshall and Glyn Williams,
*The Great Map of Mankind: British
Perceptions of the World in the Age of
Enlightenment*
(London, 1982)

Eric McCormick,
Omai: Pacific Envoy
(Auckland, 1977)

Frank McLynn,
Captain Cook: Master of the Seas
(New Haven and London, 2011)

Maria Nugent,
Botany Bay: Where Histories Meet
(Crows Nest, NSW, 2005)

Maria Nugent,
Captain Cook Was Here
(Cambridge, 2009)

Patrick O'Brian,
Joseph Banks
(London, 1987)

Dan O'Sullivan,
In Search of Captain Cook
(London, 2008)

Nigel Rigby and Pieter van der Merwe,
Captain Cook in the Pacific
(London, 2002)

John Robson,
*Captain Cook's World: Maps of the Life
and Voyages of James Cook RN*
(Auckland, 2000)

John Robson,
The Captain Cook Encyclopaedia
(London, 2004)

Anne Salmond,
*Between Worlds: Early Exchanges between
Māori and Europeans, 1773–1815*
(Auckland and London, 1997)

Anne Salmond,
*The Trial of the Cannibal Dog: Captain
Cook in the South Seas*
(London, 2003)

Anne Salmond,
*Aphrodite's Island:
The European Discovery of Tahiti*
(Berkeley and London, 2010)

Bernard Smith,
*European Vision and the
South Pacific, 1768–1850*
(Oxford, 1960)

Nicholas Thomas,
*Discoveries: The Voyages of
Captain Cook*
(London, 2003)

Glyn Williams,
*The Death of Captain Cook:
A Hero Made and Unmade*
(London, 2008)

Online Resources

Information on the British Library's
James Cook collections and exhibition
programme is available at
https://www.bl.uk/

The National Library of Australia
website has searchable editions of the
journals of Cook, Banks and Parkinson,
plus Hawkesworth's book:
http://southseas.nla.gov.au/index_
voyaging.html

The journals of Joseph Banks and
William Wales are available online via
the website of the State Library of
New South Wales at
http://www2.sl.nsw.gov.au/

Te Ara – The Encyclopedia of New Zealand
is an invaluable online resource for
Māori history and culture in the
eighteenth century:
https://teara.govt.nz/

Illustration Credits:

12 Museum of Contemporary Art, purchased with
funds provided by the Coe and Mordant families,
2006. Image courtesy of the artist and Museum of
Contemporary Art, Australia. © the artist
101 NMUM/Alamy Stock Photo
165, 166 De Agostini/Getty Images
212-213 Bridgeman Art Library/Christies Images
217 Getty Images.

Index

Page numbers in **bold** indicate a major reference; page numbers in *italics* indicate illustrations or maps. Transcriptions of indigenous names are indicated by inverted commas, eg 'Omai'.